Behind the Scenes at Boston Ballet

UNIVERSITY PRESS OF FLORIDA

Florida A&M University, Tallahassee
Florida Atlantic University, Boca Raton
Florida Gulf Coast University, Ft. Myers
Florida International University, Miami
Florida State University, Tallahassee
New College of Florida, Sarasota
University of Central Florida, Orlando
University of Florida, Gainesville
University of North Florida, Jacksonville
University of South Florida, Tampa
University of West Florida, Pensacola

University Press of Florida

Gainesville · Tallahassee

Tampa · Boca Raton

Pensacola · Orlando

Miami · Jacksonville

Ft. Myers · Sarasota

Behind the Scenes
at Boston Ballet

Christine Temin with Photos by Wally Gilbert

Text copyright 2009 by Christine Temin

Photography copyright 2009 by Wally Gilbert

Printed in the United States of America on acid-free paper

All rights reserved

14 13 12 11 10 09   6 5 4 3 2 1

Library of Congress Cataloging-in-Publication Data

Temin, Christine

Behind the scenes at Boston Ballet/Christine Temin with photos by Wally Gilbert.

p. cm.

ISBN 978-0-8130-3353-2 (alk. paper)

1. Ballet. 2. Boston Ballet. 3. Ballet companies. I. Title.

GV1787.T27 2009

792.89–dc22   2008048898

The University Press of Florida is the scholarly publishing agency for the State University System of Florida, comprising Florida A&M University, Florida Atlantic University, Florida Gulf Coast University, Florida International University, Florida State University, New College of Florida, University of Central Florida, University of Florida, University of North Florida, University of South Florida, and University of West Florida.

University Press of Florida

15 Northwest 15th Street

Gainesville, FL 32611-2079

http://www.upf.com

To the memory of my mother, Judith Nilson Woll, who took me to my first ballet performances, with stars like Nureyev and Fonteyn, who made an indelible impression.

Contents

Preface

The purpose of this book is to take readers behind the scenes into the inner workings of an American ballet company that has risen in recent years to international status. These are the stories not only of the artistic director, the choreographers, and the dancers but also of the scheduler, the wardrobe manager, the physical therapists, the pointe shoe manager, the accompanists, and others the public never hears about. It takes a huge team effort to keep a ballet company running.

This book would not have been possible without the complete—and unprecedented—cooperation of Boston Ballet's dancers and staff, starting with artistic director Mikko Nissinen and former executive director Valerie Wilder. Special thanks to Elizabeth Olds, the assistant to Nissinen. Liz, who was herself a principal dancer with the Royal Winnipeg Ballet, gave us access to rehearsals, interviews with dancers and choreographers, and dozens of other necessities for the book. She was also a great Madge, the witch in the *La Sylphide* production that Boston Ballet performed in Spain in 2007. Her talents are endless!

Wally Gilbert was greatly intrigued by the project, to the extent that he came with me to Madrid to watch the company's 2007 summer tour. His stamina and enthusiasm were unflagging, and his pictures are gorgeous.

Introduction

Ballet in Boston

"This will be the most important letter I will ever write you as you will see. My pen burns my hand as I write: words will not flow into the ink fast enough. We have a real chance to have an American ballet within 3 yrs. time. When I say ballet—I mean a trained company of young dancers—not Russians—but Americans with Russian stars to start with—a company superior to the dregs of the old Diaghilev Company. . . .

"We have the future in our hands. For Christ's sweet sake let us honor it" (Nicholas Weber, *Patron Saints: Five Rebels Who Opened America to a New Art, 1928 to 1943* [New York: Alfred A. Knopf, 1992], 179–80).

These words are the beginning and end of a sixteen-page letter written in 1933 by Lincoln Kirstein, a wealthy, young, well-connected, and Harvard-educated Bostonian, to his friend A. Everett "Chick" Austin Jr., the visionary young director of the Wadsworth Atheneum in Hartford, Connecticut. The eventual result of the impassioned missive was the arrival in America of George Balanchine, the greatest classical choreographer of the twentieth century. And that arrival led, with many bumps along the way, to the New York City Ballet, "the greatest performing arts institution of our time," as the late Ford Foundation vice president W. McNeil Lowry described it to me in the 1980s. It was thanks in large part to Lowry that, in 1963, the Ford Foundation distributed $7.7 million to jump-start several American ballet companies.

Several decades on, classical dance in America is in trouble. A very few organizations, including the New York City Ballet and San Francisco

Ballet, continue to get by, banking on large endowments accumulated in a more prosperous past, and in a few other cities regular support has provided lesser companies with reasonable financial security. But ballet is not a real presence in most of the United States, as it is in Europe, where most cities of any size have a suitable opera house, which Boston does not.

Tickets to American ballet are hard to sell and generally so expensive, often at $100 or so a seat, that middle-income Americans can't afford to go. Classical choreographers of real merit are few. While dancers' technical virtuosity soars, their expressiveness diminishes, in part because of the dearth of careful, detailed coaching that requires many hours in the studio and more money than most companies can spend.

This book is about Boston Ballet, an American company that has never had financial security and that has had a checkered history, economically and sometimes artistically, since its 1958 founding by a determined suburban ballet teacher, E. Virginia Williams. It was called the New England Civic Ballet then, part of the country's burgeoning regional ballet movement.

Its home is in a city that, if not the Athens of America, as it likes to think of itself, is at least the academic capital of America, probably home to more Nobel Prize winners per capita than any other city in the world and to two of the country's preeminent arts institutions, both founded in the nineteenth century, the Boston Symphony Orchestra and the Museum of Fine Arts, Boston. It is, at the same time, a city that Lincoln Kirstein fled as soon as possible, expressing his feelings about Boston's stuffy society with the line "Harvard thinks of the arts as a playpen for young gentlemen" (interview with author in the November/December 1981 issue of *Harvard Magazine*).

The New England Civic Ballet was able to make the transition to Boston Ballet, a professional company, in 1963 because it was one of eight organizations that shared the Ford Foundation money. Balanchine was involved in selecting the recipients, generally companies in his orbit, coast to coast. The result was that American ballet then and now is still dominated by the work and style of Balanchine, who died in 1983.

I have followed Boston Ballet since its founding by Williams, and I wrote about it from 1978 to 2005 as dance critic for the *Boston Globe*. I draw on that experience here, but the focus of this book is not the company's history. Its aim is to tell the story of the many people whose talent, creativity, and plain and often painful hard work is necessary in order to produce seasons of first-class ballet—from the directors, choreographers, dancers, and musicians who receive the all too occasional publicity in the popular press, to the répétiteurs, rehearsal pianists, set designers, physical therapists, and others the public rarely hears about.

In its sheer ambition and work ethic, Boston Ballet is exceptionally strong, but it is also, sadly, an example of America's lack of financial support for the arts. The company receives virtually no money from its city or state and, in contrast to Boston's older cultural institutions, founded by the city's elite, relatively little from its citizens. It has yet to attract to its board enough members for whom supporting the ballet is more than a civic duty or a way to build their social résumés. When I interviewed Boston Ballet trustees for this book, two of them could not name their favorite ballets from the previous season. The company also lacks adequate support from balletomanes who, working from memories of a decade or more ago, when the company was at its weakest, seldom attend Boston Ballet performances, and from a broader audience who have yet to be shown why ballet is worth their time and money.

Yet, despite its financial troubles, Boston Ballet has developed an ensemble and repertoire that preserve and promote ballet as few other companies are doing. In addition to performing the standard repertory at a high level, Boston is finally establishing a clear identity through the ballets by its house choreographer, Jorma Elo, by Helen Pickett, a newcomer of considerable talent, and by young members of the company itself.

In a number of other countries, ballet is a fixture outside the cultural capital. Balletomanes in Canada have several choices of fine companies, from Toronto to Montreal to Winnipeg. Ditto in Germany, where companies in Stuttgart and Frankfurt are destinations for ballet-goers. In France, it's not just the Paris Opera offering top quality work but Marseilles and other cities as well. If the United States is to establish a similar tradition and build on the "American ballet" that Kirstein started, not only companies in New York and San Francisco but also those like the Boston Ballet must flourish. At it current high level of performance, it deserves to.

Eve Rounds, a Boston Ballet trustee trained as a dancer, articulated part of the problem. "Ballet is so fragile and ephemeral. The world is about tangibility. It's tough to get people to understand that an ephemeral art is worthy, even though it's not a painting that you buy at auction and hang on the wall. You have to change people's views about what value is."

American ballet needs a few more Lincoln Kirsteins, knowledgeable, determined, and passionate. But Kirstein represented a combination of access to money and passion for dance that is lamentably rare these days. It's uncertain whether the kind of talent and determination of choreographers, dancers, and other staff that I describe here will suffice to keep ballet alive in this country beyond New York and San Francisco.

Injuries and Opportunities

It's January 7, 2006. "Larissa broke her fifth metatarsal yesterday," Mikko Nissinen says in a tone of voice others might use to say, "Larissa has a cold." Larissa is Larissa Ponomarenko, the senior female principal dancer on the roster of Boston Ballet, the company Nissinen directs. Nissinen's apparent nonchalance about the condition of one of his finest ballerinas comes from having spent three-quarters of his life in the ballet world, where someone is always breaking a fifth metatarsal. (It's the bone that runs from the midfoot to the base of the small toe, and it takes much of the stress of repeated landings from jumps and pirouettes.) Ponomarenko's broken foot means that she will be out at least for the troupe's two March programs. She was supposed to have danced the lead on the opening night of the company's 2006 spring season, in Sir Frederick Ashton's version of *La Fille mal gardée* (The Wayward Daughter). Instead, she was replaced by Lorna Feijóo, who was herself already suffering a stress reaction in a bone.

As a precaution for the following program, a mixed bill in which Feijóo's participation was even more essential, Nissinen had Misa Kuranaga, a 23-year-old dancer in her third season with the Ballet, take over Feijóo's second scheduled performance. Kuranaga—tiny, fresh, even childlike while also possessed of a dazzling technique—looked as though Ashton had created *Fille* specifically for her, although his version of the classic dates from 1960, more than two decades before she was born.

Ponomarenko was valiant during the March programs, arriving at the theater limping, her right foot encased in a supportive "boot," to watch her colleagues dance the roles she had planned to perform. "I love the ballet," she said. "So what else can I do?"

"One dancer's injury is another dancer's opportunity," Nissinen remarked. "That's how most of us got where we are." He wasn't being callous. He was being realistic.

The real world of classical dance is more dramatic than *The Turning Point, The Red Shoes,* and all the other ballet movies ever made. In its relatively short history, Boston Ballet has faced charges of racism; cases of dancer anorexia; even a young dancer's death, with blame temporarily laid on the company, along with the precipitous, publicly embarrassing departures of one director and one director-elect. The real story, though, lies not in these occasional public incidents but in the daily challenges of preparing and performing a repertory that spans almost two centuries, from the 1836 *La Sylphide* to works created for the company today.

Although classical ballet has its origins in the European court dance of the sixteenth and seventeenth centuries, when it was about monarchs and nobles preening rather than sweating, in its modern form it has become not only the most physically challenging of the arts but more demanding than all but intentionally masochistic sports. Nonetheless, ballet is an art, not a sport, and so must combine demanding physical technique with varying degrees of choreographic creativity, musical expertise, dramatic flair, and the taste to fuse them together—all within a budget dictated by the public's limited taste for the fine arts and the historically limited role of ballet in this country.

PART ONE

The Elements

1

The Artistic Director

In its nearly half-century existence as a professional company, Boston Ballet has had but five artistic directors: its founder, E. Virginia Williams, followed by Violette Verdy, Bruce Marks, Anna-Marie Holmes, and Mikko Nissinen.

Williams, who died in 1984 at age 70, was the pioneer, a role she inherited partly from adventurous ancestors, including one who came to America on the ship after the *Mayflower*. Her ballet education was initially sketchy. She took classes with any professional who turned up in Boston, including the Italians who performed with the Boston Opera. There was no American Ballet Theatre or New York City Ballet when she was growing up, no great company for her to aspire to.

Balanchine became her mentor. She would go to New York to see him teach, and she devoted her career to teaching in his style. Once he had established a stable company, he, in turn, poached her most talented dancers for his own troupe.

Verdy, a generation younger than Williams, had good training in her native France, then a great career with New York City Ballet and a stormy experience as artistic director of the Paris Opera Ballet in the late 1970s. She and Williams were directors of Boston Ballet from 1980 until 1983, when Williams retired. On that occasion Verdy answered a question about future repertoire with the firm position that "we have to take care of the endowment of the classics." Williams had had her company perform works by modern choreographers, including Merce Cunningham and Paul Taylor. Verdy said that the Ballet would add "a few new exciting things, but they are not really the point, though, for a classical company" (interview with the author in the *Boston Globe,* April 3, 1983).

They were very much the point for her successor, Bruce Marks, whose initial training was in modern dance. Marks brought in dances by top modern choreographers, a list headed by Mark Morris. Marks had been married to the Danish ballerina Toni Lander and had performed with her in the Royal Danish Ballet. So work by Denmark's greatest choreographer, August Bournonville (1805–79), also entered Boston's repertoire.

After Marks departed in 1997, Anna-Marie Holmes was appointed artistic director without an external search, a controversial move at the time. She had worked with the company in various capacities since 1985. Holmes's claim to fame was that she had been the first North American to dance with the fabled Kirov in Leningrad, which was possible in those cold war times because she was a Canadian rather than a U.S. citizen. When she took over in Boston, Holmes imported teachers, coaches, and dancers from the Soviet Union, including Natalia Dudinskaya, who had been her principal teacher in Leningrad, and she promoted the Russian-style training she had learned there. She departed in 2000 when her contract ran out.

The Ballet at that time was at a low point, both artistically and financially. In 2002 "the company wasn't seen as stable," said Valerie Wilder, its executive director from 2002 through 2008. "I thought maybe it was 'Mission Impossible.' I also thought maybe it would be very interesting because there was so much to tackle. Everybody told me that the board ate their young. They supported the artistic director but not the company as a whole. The dancers were not that good. The programming left a lot to be desired. Ben Stevenson's *Cleopatra* was the worst of the 'name-brand' ballets they were dancing. The other repertory had no point of view. It's not always even a matter of cost. It's taste, too."

The Finnish-born Mikko Nissinen arrived in Boston in 2001. He had danced with San Francisco Ballet and gone on to direct first the Marin Ballet in San Rafael, California, and then the Alberta Ballet in Calgary, Canada. He was seen as savior and stabilizer of the Boston troupe. Once he set to work, improvements in company morale and the level of dancing were almost immediate. While he hired and fired liberally, he was always clear about why.

Nissinen was born in Helsinki into a family of artists in 1962, a year

Mikko Nissinen, artistic director of Boston Ballet. Photo by Wally Gilbert.

before the birth of Boston Ballet as a professional company. His father is a painter, his mother is a ceramist, and his grandfather was a professional clarinetist trained at the Sibelius Academy, named for the composer who is a national hero in Finland.

"The biggest form of support my parents gave me," Nissinen says, "was not putting up any roadblocks in my career." When he was growing up in Helsinki, there was no single institution in Finland where dance and academic training were under the same roof, as they are in many

European countries. "Ballet was just an after-school activity," he recalls. But the training did give him the opportunity to dance with the Finnish National Opera and Ballet, up to twenty-four performances a month. In the 1970s, the Finnish Ballet established its first all-boys class. He joined the class at age 11 and made such steady progress that he became a member of the Finnish National Ballet when he was just 15. His first professional role was in a version of Richard Strauss's symphonic poem, *Til Eulenspiegel's Merry Pranks*. "My partner was heavier than I was," he says. "I was very skinny." He was, however, a natural performer. "I could never wait for the curtain to go up. I didn't have any idea of stage fright." Along the way, he started reading books on Buddhism, including one with advice that Nissinen paraphrases for his dancers: "It's okay to have butterflies in your stomach—as long as they fly in formation."

Nissinen and Jorma Elo met at the school and became fast friends. In 1979–80 they spent a "finishing" year at the Kirov Ballet School. They were in the institution that had produced male stars including Nijinsky, Nureyev, and Baryshnikov. "I had a great year there," Nissinen says. "My teacher, Oleg Sokolov, made me the class pet. I was the Prince in *The Nutcracker* on the Kirov stage when I was 17." As this comment suggests, Nissinen does not fit the stereotype of the Finn as a modest person of few words, hardly the sort to tout his accomplishments. "It's because my ancestors were from the Keralia Province of Finland," he says, "which is very near the Russian border. People from Keralia are more outgoing than other Finns."

He is the first to admit that his academic education is less illustrious than his education in dance. Some of his high school studies were through correspondence courses in Finland. He never went to college. He is, however, an autodidact. "I'd make up courses and teach them to myself," he says. He is particularly knowledgeable in fields related to ballet, including dance history and the history of art. He is also an expert in deep-sea fishing, his major passion outside the realm of the arts, and after getting his moorings in Boston, he treated himself to the purchase of a Boston Whaler Outrage 285 Walk Around (a powerboat for fishing that is presumably less cumbersome than its name.)

His training in Finland and Leningrad was in the style codified by Agrippina Vaganova. She danced with the Maryinsky, as the Kirov company was called in pre-Soviet times, from 1897 to 1916. She held several notable teaching posts in Leningrad, was artistic director of the Kirov

Ballet from 1931 to 1937, and died in Leningrad in 1951. Vaganova advocated an amalgam of the athleticism of the Italians and the soft arms and shoulders of the French. This was the only style Nissinen studied while in Finland and the Soviet Union. "It emphasized strength, theatricality, and virtuoso feats," he says. It was all he knew until he joined the Dutch National Ballet for two years and then the Basel Ballet for three. Both were strong in the more advanced sorts of European ballet, but also on Balanchine. It was Nissinen's first major encounter with the works of the master.

Ballet, it is often said, is the hardest of the arts to preserve. Nissinen is aware of that. "From the time I was in the Dutch National Ballet, I kept a journal of everything I danced. I started it because older dancers would say to me, 'I didn't keep my programs. I don't have any record of what I did.' I was determined not to be like that." So in Holland he bought a videocassette tape recorder. "I built a base library of ballet video tapes," he says. "I've been adding to them ever since." At one time he had more than 850 tapes.

He had already fallen in love with American dance by the time Helgi Tomasson, director of the San Francisco Ballet, invited him to San Francisco to talk about becoming a member of that company. "I took one class and then we sorted out the details," Nissinen says, making the whole procedure sound simple. In moving to San Francisco, he became a member of the oldest surviving ballet company in the country, established in 1933, fifteen years before New York City Ballet. He would be far more deeply immersed in Balanchine than he would at the Dutch National or Basel Ballet. The Icelandic-born Tomasson had been a principal dancer with Balanchine's company from 1970 to 1985, mastering its repertoire before heading west. San Francisco Ballet acquired not only many Balanchine ballets but also the complex Balanchine style, which can amount to tongue-twisters for the feet. Among the Balanchine ballets Nissinen danced during his ten years at SFB were *Theme and Variations, Ballo della Regina,* and *Tchaikovsky Pas de Deux.* He got as complete an education in Balanchine as he would have had in the master's own company—perhaps even more complete, as New York City Ballet after Balanchine was having problems of its own in maintaining its legacy while continuing to grow.

"I consider San Francisco Ballet my home company," Nissinen says. "It's where I learned the most. I appreciate the value system there. The dancing Helgi wants is clean and clear, with no show-off stuff. It's not Broadway.

"Helgi wasn't very talkative during my years as a dancer there." (Nor is he in general.) "But he told Boston Ballet that I was the right person for this job." Before Boston, Nissinen honed his directorial skills at the Marin Ballet and then in Alberta. (His appointment in Boston came so suddenly that he commuted between Boston and Calgary for his first year as Boston's and last year as Alberta's artistic director.) "I always knew I wanted to be a director. In Finland I looked at the director there and I thought, 'Is that all? Shouldn't he be doing more?' There was no nurturing of the dancers."

Bizarre circumstances brought Nissinen to Boston. In September 2000, the Ballet board announced that it had hired Maina Gielgud to replace Holmes. Gielgud had spent fourteen years successfully building the Australian Ballet, and then had a shorter and tumultuous tenure as artistic director of the Royal Danish Ballet. Her uncle was the celebrated British actor Sir John Gielgud, and her great-aunt was the even more legendary actress Dame Ellen Terry. These glamorous associations were not lost on the Boston trustees. Also not lost on them was the fact that during her years at the Australian Ballet she had turned what was essentially a provincial company into one of international stature, which performed at Covent Garden in London and the Metropolitan Opera House in New York, major stages on which Boston's board would love to see their company appear.

Holmes said at the time that she was told by the Boston Ballet board not to show up at the September press conference that introduced Gielgud as artistic director designate. So she crashed the party, presenting Gielgud with a bouquet of flowers. By May 2001, however, Gielgud was so frustrated by her differences with the trustees, chiefly financial, that she fled Boston, saying she could work within a strict budget, but that the board refused to give her a specific figure so she could begin planning her first season. Jonathan McPhee, the company's longtime music director, was named interim artistic coordinator, and chief ballet master Jorden Morris, previously with the Royal Winnipeg Ballet, dealt with the dancers during this rocky period.

Probably neither Gielgud nor Nissinen would have endorsed the stated mission of the board chairman, James Wilson, who announced at various times that Boston Ballet was going to be one of the five greatest classical troupes in the world within five years. Sometimes he substituted the number ten, but either way it sounded like a Soviet-style plan to build a better tractor. It takes time, money, and taste to leap into ballet's Top Ten. Five years, even ten years, aren't enough, especially when the board is not prepared to provide enough money to achieve this unrealistically ambitious goal.

In hiring Nissinen, though, Boston Ballet got a director with rare taste and ambition. Gielgud was better known than Nissinen in international circles, partly because of her famous name, but also for what she accomplished in Australia. Both Gielgud and Nissinen had fine credentials first as performers and then as directors, but their aesthetic preferences are almost opposites. Nissinen loves Balanchine and contemporary works, especially those of Morris, Elo, and Pickett, while Gielgud's greatest dancing years were with Maurice Béjart, a European whose generally flamboyant and flashy style and choreography are anathema to many American critics, myself included. (A member of the Mark Morris camp once joked in conversation with me about what he called "Euro-trash" ballet. "There's always something in the beginning, like maybe a red high-heeled shoe that falls from the rafters," he said. "That's how you know you're in for something *meaningful*.") For Boston Ballet's board to select two potential directors with such extremely different aesthetics in such a short period suggests that the board had little idea of what kind of ballet company it wanted.

Would Nissinen ever have a Béjart work for Boston Ballet? He hesitates at the question, as he doesn't when talking about acquiring more works by Balanchine or Elo. "Why not?" he finally replies. "It would just have to be a specific piece, though, maybe *Song of a Wayfarer*." A dark piece for two men, set to Gustav Mahler's *Lieder eines fahrenden Gesellen, Song* is atypically simple and stripped down in Béjart's oeuvre, letting the music set the tone.

By the end of the spring 2008 season, planning future repertoire was hardly Nissinen's primary concern. The company was in financial straits, struggling with a debt of $8 million, largely the result of its 2004 eviction from the Wang Theatre for its annual run of *The Nutcracker*, the holiday ballet that pays the bills for most American companies. The company was forced to make severe cuts in the number of dancers and staff. For his part, Nissinen made it a priority to improve the board.

One of Nissinen's primary goals on arriving in Boston was to start the company touring again to increase its visibility to international audiences. The troupe had been off the international touring circuit for well over a decade. In the summer of 2007 Nissinen was able to pull off a lengthy tour to festivals in Spain, a great boost to company morale. Determined to keep the dancers traveling, Nissinen announced another tour for August 2008, this time to Korea and Tokyo. But the arrangements for Tokyo didn't work out. So the company would travel halfway around the world for just four performances in Seoul, spending more time in the air than on the stage.

Ironically, with all the depressing events of 2008, the company had never danced better.

2

The Executive Director

When Valerie Wilder was appointed executive director of the National Ballet of Canada in 1996, she became the first woman in North America to hold that position in a major ballet company. It's the same title she held at Boston Ballet from 2002 to 2008.

Her education was a model of ingenuity and enterprise. To a certain extent, she says, it happened because "my parents were 'hands-off.' They told me I was born as an adult." So she traipsed around three continents—North America, Europe, and Asia—seeking the dance training she knew she needed in order to join a major company. At the same time she was also attending high school, college, and graduate school.

Born in Pasadena, California, Wilder traveled to Kobe, near Osaka, with her parents, who were teachers and missionaries. She was enrolled in Japanese public school and started ballet lessons there. She then traveled to London's Royal Ballet School in the era of Fonteyn and Nureyev. Both she and her parents had understood from the Royal's literature that she could continue her high school education there. She couldn't. "I discovered that the academic program wasn't really available due to lack of interest on the part of the dance students." Given the choice between working on leg extensions and pirouettes or studying algebra, a ballet-bound teenager will usually choose the former.

But Wilder was uncomfortable with not having a high school diploma, so back she went to Japan to pack two years of academics into one. Her parents persuaded her to accept a scholarship to Butler University in Indianapolis. There she performed with a student dance group while the biochemistry department tried to woo her into a career in science. She stayed at Butler for two years, then went to Toronto to join the National Ballet of Canada in 1970. Her first job, ironically, was to perform with the company on a tour to Japan for Expo '70 in Osaka. The Canadian company did a lot of touring, sometimes as a backdrop for Rudolf Nureyev (which Boston also did, in order to be able to tour). In one such season, Wilder danced 108 *Swan Lake*s with the Toronto troupe on a tour presented by legendary impresario Sol Hurok.

Along the way, Wilder's interests began to veer toward the business side of ballet. "It was thought at the time that if you focused on anything but ballet your career was diminished," she says. "But while performing with the National Ballet, I became a union representative for the dancers, and I took university courses in cost accounting and business management. If you're a union rep sitting across the table from a board member who runs a multimillion-dollar company, you want to be prepared. I started doing my own income taxes, which was unheard of in the ballet world. Then I was doing the whole company's taxes. Then I started doing contract negotiations." Finally, in 1976, while she was still dancing, she and her husband, Geoffrey Perry, formed Perry and Wilder Incorporated to manage the business affairs of more than 100 artists. One of them was the legendary Danish dancer Erik Bruhn. "I talked to him every day from 1976 on. I stopped dancing in the early 1980s. In 1983 Erik was offered the artistic directorship of the National Ballet of Canada. He said he would take it if I came with him as his second in command. So I was back at the National Ballet with the title 'artistic administrator.'" After Bruhn's death in 1986, Wilder became artistic director and later coartistic director, leading the company on tours to New York City, Washington, D.C., London, and Germany, a schedule that no Boston Ballet artistic director has yet to equal. (Both Maina Gielgud and Wilder were able to achieve international tours at prime international venues partly because of funding from the Australian and Canadian governments, the kind of funding Boston Ballet lacks.)

In 1996 Wilder became the executive director of the National Ballet. By now accustomed to doing two things at once, she also enrolled at McGill University in Montreal, earning a master's degree in management. "Corporations spend tons of money on how to run businesses," she says, "but nonprofits don't." McGill, though, had a whole division for people who ran nonprofits, with a mature and experienced faculty. "It was a truly life-changing opportunity."

This mix of academics and dance, trying not to shortchange either, was her first unusual career move. Most ballet dancers skip or postpone attending universities because of the urgency of their short careers. "Almost no one in Boston Ballet has gone to college," Wilder says. But at 30 or 35, most of them will be ready to retire from the stage, either staying in the ballet world as teachers, coaches, or choreographers or going to college to try something different. There are any number of college and university programs to accommodate them. Thirty is now an acceptable age to start college and a new career, and ballet dancers are generally well equipped for the switch. They're extremely well disciplined, and they hold dozens of roles in their heads. They are good higher-education candidates, even for the most prestigious colleges and universities in the nation. Boston Ballet has seen several dancers leave the company to attend Brown University in Providence, which has extremely competitive admissions. Boston Ballet dancers have gone on to careers in fields ranging from real estate to public relations.

Wilder doesn't remember precisely how she met Nissinen. "I probably hired him to be a guest artist with the National Ballet," she says. "I'd seen him in galas in Montreal and Stuttgart. He always had questions about how things ran. I remember saying to Erik Bruhn, 'I think there's a future director there.' While Mikko was in Alberta, he lost two executive directors, so he took over that job, too."

Wilder had ideas that some ballet people, including Nissinen, would consider radical. They include the number of performances the company should give. "The assumption used to be that if you do a show you should do as many performances as possible, to give dancers as many chances as possible to be onstage. By the time I got here Boston Ballet had worked themselves into a state where they did twelve performances of every program." (*The Nutcracker* was, of course, performed dozens of times each season.) "When American Ballet Theatre does the big full-length ballets at the Metropolitan Opera House, they only do seven or eight performances," Wilder says. "It would never cross their minds to do more.

"In the 2002–03 season, companies in Toronto, New York, and Stuttgart all did *Onegin*, as did Boston Ballet." (*Onegin* is choreographer John Cranko's masterful reworking of Pushkin's novel in verse.) "In every city there was a total attendance of 16,000 to 18,000. Stuttgart did seven performances in a 1,700-seat house. We did twelve performances in that huge theater [the Wang in Boston], which has 3,600 seats. So if the same number of people will attend with fewer performances, why incur the unnecessary expense of additional nights in the theater? My goal when I got here was to reduce the number of shows. We differentiated between programs that would run for one week or two weeks." The one-week programs, generally the more experimental ones or triple bills of one-act classics, now run for just six performances; the two-week programs run for ten or eleven performances.

The downside of this scenario, in effect in the past few seasons, is that choreographers are creating new works that will be danced only six times in their debut year. After that, if a new work has been successful, it may be repeated in a couple of years, while the Ballet still owns the rights to it. But the initial six performances are barely enough for the dancers to become comfortable with the choreography, much less to wear it like a second skin. Nissinen and the dancers are, understandably, unhappy with the small numbers of performances. "I made a deal with Valerie," he says, "that we would make it up with touring."

"That restructuring of the seasons was hard for subscribers," Wilder acknowledges. Subscribers get the best seats in the house, and with fewer performances, some were demoted to lesser seats. At its peak, Boston Ballet had around 10,000 subscribers. The number dropped to around 7,000, but by the end of the 2007–08 season, the figure was back up to around 9,000, thanks in part to clever marketing initiatives (e.g., "Take your date to *Romeo and Juliet* for half price").

In 2002, the year she accepted the executive director post, Wilder says that Boston Ballet "was thought of in the industry as quite a troubled company. There hadn't been a full-time artistic director [Nissinen was still commuting to Alberta] nor an executive director for a year. It was an issue of infrastructure and support."

When Wilder became executive director in Boston, "the search process that had produced Maina Gielgud, only to have her disappear, just added to the perception of instability," Wilder says. "The tragedy that happened with Heidi Guenther also looked bad." In 1997, while on a family excursion to Disneyland, Guenther, a 22-year-old Boston Ballet corps member, suddenly died. At first it looked like the result of an eating disorder, the kind from which so many young female ballet dancers across the country have suffered. The cause of death was eventually judged to be a heart attack, but first the Ballet endured a barrage of bad press.

Before Boston's board hired Wilder, Nissinen says he had asked for, and received, veto power over the candidates for executive director, and he was wary of the power-sharing aspect of Wilder's role. Their names would be on the same line in official company documents and in programs, and they would each earn a six-figure salary that Nissinen said was the same for the two. According to the company's tax return for 2005, though, Wilder received $306,025, whereas the figure for Nissinen was $226,025.

"We have a dual leadership structure," Wilder says. "Both Mikko and I report directly to the board. This model is now common in America, with the executive director handling such areas as finance, marketing, and development. I also deal with unions, utilities, and health care. The reality is that the executive and artistic directors have to work closely together. Mikko and I do that as well as any duo." They speak daily. Their offices are on the same floor of the company's building, a couple of doors apart. "We seem to see eye-to-eye on what we like artistically and on what we would like to see happen here," Wilder says. "When we can't afford something, Mikko is usually a reasonable partner."

I first interviewed Wilder for this book in the autumn of 2007. By March 2008 she was no longer any kind of partner at all. She and Boston Ballet board chairman Richard Davis issued a terse joint statement announcing that she was leaving. "I am exploring a number of exciting opportunities in the nonprofit world," she said.

"There isn't enough room here to grow," she said after her resignation. "Boston Ballet is so busy just with its own survival. The Board needs to participate more in making the case for the Ballet with the leaders in the community in finance and government. Some of the Board members have those contacts, but not all of them. That whole game needs to step up and improve. The Board needs to make a case for Boston Ballet in the community. Boston Ballet needs a transformational gift to go on," she said, citing the "transformational" figure as at least $10 million.

Soon after her resignation she accepted the post of executive director of the Australian Ballet, which, like the National Ballet of Canada, has substantial government support, which puts it on a different financial footing from Boston Ballet. Boston gives about 85 performances a year. Australia gives about 200, with high-profile tours in Europe and regular appearances in several Australian venues, including Sydney's iconic Opera House. Whatever the challenges of a national ballet, they do not include the fund-raising that made her position in Boston such a frustrating one.

3

The Challenges

Only four days after Wilder's departure announcement, the *New York Times* reported another blow to the Ballet. Because of its financial problems, it would cut nearly 20 percent of its dancers for the 2008–2009 season (Daniel J. Wakin, *New York Times,* March 14, 2008). Over the previous few seasons, the company had already downsized its administrative staff by 40 percent, Nissinen said. Now the number of dancers would shrink from fifty to forty-one. Nissinen told the *New York Times* that he would make up the loss for large productions by hiring freelancers and drawing on the members of Boston Ballet II, the company's junior wing. It wasn't lost on Boston Ballet watchers that freelancers wouldn't have trained with the company and couldn't be expected to fit instantly into the style that Nissinen had so carefully cultivated during his directorship. And the dancers in BB II are presumably not in the main company because they're not yet ready for it. Putting on a brave show, Nissinen said of the cuts, "My goal and aim is that it doesn't affect the quality of the artistic product."

Boston Ballet's fiscal condition is primarily the responsibility of the executive director and the board of trustees, but it provides the backdrop for every significant decision made by Nissinen, himself a persuasive and energetic fund-raiser. The company's current situation reflects the problems common to ballet companies in America as well as the idiosyncrasies of Boston.

Boston

The strengths and weaknesses of Boston Ballet in some respects reflect its home. Boston is a music town, renowned for a number of superb musical organizations, the list led by the Boston Symphony Orchestra. This makes for a surplus of well-trained freelance musicians. And that means that the Boston Ballet Orchestra is not only one of the best of its kind in the country but also one of the city's largest musical ensembles.

Boston is also a medical town, home of Children's Hospital Boston, the Massachusetts General Hospital, and other distinguished institutions. So Boston Ballet has an on-site dancers' clinic that is a satellite of Children's and a model for other ballet clinics worldwide.

The Boston area is an intellectual haven, the home of Harvard, MIT, and many other colleges and universities. Unfortunately, that doesn't necessarily make for a big dance audience. It can indeed lead to a bit of snobbery, with faculty at world-class universities who might seem to be a natural audience for ballet feeling that only the world's most prestigious dance companies are worth their arts dollar. The last time I saw a substantial Harvard presence at a ballet performance in Boston was in 1981, when New York City Ballet came to town with a menu of Balanchine "leotard" ballets.

Boston is also a class-conscious town, dating from the days when the Brahmins, the old Yankee upper class, and the Irish immigrants had little relationship except that of master and servant. By the late nineteenth century, however, the Irish controlled city hall. The Brahmins wanted their privacy and exclusivity, so early on the city's cultural institutions did not ask local government for money. The Museum of Fine Arts didn't want city funding when it was founded in the 1870s, preferring to maintain its clubby air. That model has worked for the old-line institutions, although they're all now offering "outreach" programs, but it has deprived newer arts organizations of critical public financial support. Boston Ballet would take money from almost any legal source. The city gives it $2,500—that's right, no more zeroes—every other year.

Eviction!

In 2004 Boston Ballet had to face what was at the time the most serious crisis in its history. The company was booted out of its performing home, the Wang Theatre, for its annual run of *The Nutcracker,* so that the Wang could try to enrich its own coffers by substituting the *Radio City Christmas Spectacular,* starring the Rockettes. (Along with the smaller Shubert Theatre across the street, the Wang is now part of the so-called Citi Performing Arts Center, named after its current sponsor.) The Wang, a renovated movie theater with poor sightlines and acoustics, is not a suitable setting for dance anyway, but performing *Nutcracker* in it was critical to the Ballet's finances.

Until the eviction, ticket sales from *Nutcracker* had kept Boston Ballet dancing for much of the rest of the year, as *Nutcracker* revenue does for most American ballet troupes. Moving from the 3,600-seat Wang to two other Boston theaters, first the 1,600-seat Colonial in 2004, then the 2,600-seat Opera House in 2005, meant losses that had a ripple effect, causing Nissinen to make cutbacks and compromises in the company's repertory. *Nutcracker'*s eviction caused Boston Ballet to hemorrhage money: it took a $4 million hit in lost revenues the first year and $2 million a year thereafter. By the end of 2007, the total debt had grown to $8 million.

In the same year that Boston Ballet's *Nutcracker* was kicked out of the Wang for its financially critical performances, New York City Ballet was threatened with eviction from the Saratoga Performing Arts Center, its summer home in upstate New York for nearly four decades. New Yorkers, including public officials, raised such an outcry that SPAC had to back down. City Ballet stayed put. Nothing like that happened in Boston.

The company's eviction from the Wang came at a challenging time for American ballet companies generally. The business of ballet is now also faring poorly in cities other than Boston, Valerie Wilder notes. "We've all been seeing some resistance [to high ticket prices]. In ballet, many companies are experiencing a structural deficit." The *Nutcracker* debacle "threatened the life of the organization," she adds. "It was shocking." The company got the bad news just over a year ahead of time, in the fall of 2003. "That sounds like a long time," Wilder says. "But it's not in terms of booking a theater. We knew there was too much dependence on

Nutcracker. We thought we'd have five to ten years to adjust that imbalance. What we didn't need was for it all to happen overnight. It certainly got me out meeting people and visiting other theaters immediately."

Boston Ballet's eviction from the Wang was especially galling in light of the other uses made of that building. The Wang's decision to throw out *Nutcracker* in favor of the Rockettes dressed as reindeer is consistent with its run of musicals like *Starlight Express* and *Big River* and other Broadway retreads and its bonus to its president and CEO, Josiah Spaulding Jr., of $1,265,000 (on top of a salary of $409,000, reduced from more than $500,000 in previous years) while the organization was cutting in half the budget of Shakespeare on the Common, which the Wang Center also presents (see Geoff Edgers, "Amid Struggles, Arts Center Chief Got $1.2m Bonus," *Boston Globe*, July 31, 2007). The Wang's tax-exempt status seems a questionable fit given the diet of recycled Broadway shows and other pop fare it offers and its generous compensation of its CEO.

In light of the consequences of the Boston Ballet's eviction from the Wang, and the sympathetic hearing it would have received in many quarters concerned about the Wang's pandering programming, the company made what seems an odd decision. Instead of making a public fuss over the Wang's action, the Ballet decided to swallow the awful news and not start an open dispute with another nonprofit. "The jury is still out on that decision," Wilder said. "At the time, we didn't want to look as if we were about to go under, but the truth of the matter is that the situation was dire."

Real Estate Problems

"Boston Ballet is the only company of any size or stature in North America that does not perform in a purpose-built theater," Wilder says. For Houston, San Francisco, Seattle, and Miami, "having their own buildings gives them a permanent tangible presence in their cities. Aside from the lack of city funding, this is the single biggest disadvantage the company endures compared with our peers. Since many of these specialized theaters are city-owned buildings that subsidize their nonprofit tenants, we pay higher rent than most companies. Our theater situation also prevents us from controlling customer relationships and, fundamentally, the entire experience in the theater."

Theaters that are true homes to their city's ballet companies also tend to be adjacent to or near the studios where the companies rehearse, or they even house those studios, which is a huge advantage. Boston Ballet's South End studio building, on the other hand, is a fifteen-block hike from the Wang, and every time the company performs there it means the transfer of eighty-six people who work in the Clarendon Street building—dancers, artistic staff, choreographers, ballet masters and mistresses, the company pianist, and conductor, plus transport from the company warehouse of the sets and costumes. Then, one or two weeks later, everyone and everything moves back. This massive, expensive transfer happens half a dozen times a year.

Consider the difference between this constant back-and-forth and the situation of companies that can occupy their theaters for months at a time. This availability allows these companies to create repertory seasons. There's a Program A, B, C, etc., and the combinations mix and match for many weeks. This allows the dancers to try again if they weren't pleased with their first take on a ballet, and it allows audiences a chance to revisit a ballet in performance with other works on other programs. Visiting out-of-town balletomanes can see three different programs on three successive nights. For the season, the dancers don't have to move out of their dressing rooms; the costumes and sets don't have to be packed up and unpacked. The dancers in San Francisco and City Ballet have homes. Boston's dancers have a revolving door.

The problems with the Wang didn't stop with its distance from the company's studios. The Wang is a movie palace dating from the Roaring Twenties, which accounts for its gaudy gilded décor and its minimal rake and distant balconies. Audiences' eyes were supposed to be trained on the center of a huge screen where a movie was playing, not on the stage below. Even after much renovation, today's audiences still play a game of leaning this way and that to see dancers on the stage rather than the head in front of them. And that's after paying $110 for a top single price ticket. (The lowest price for single tickets is $25.) The Wang's approximately 3,600 seats include a 1,535-seat balcony that is often used by the Ballet only for staff or student seating.

Boston has a model that the Ballet would love to emulate. The city's Institute for Contemporary Art was formerly housed in an old police station in the Back Bay that was an awkward space at best and had to close for long periods between shows because there was no back-of-house storage. The Institute raised $65 million for a splendid new $51 million building that opened in 2006 and for an endowment to support it. The new museum was designed by the radical New York architects Diller Scofidio + Renfro, whose previous ventures had included "Blur," a temporary structure in Switzerland made entirely of fog. The new ICA has a 325-seat theater for chamber-sized performances, for which Boston Ballet has no suitable facility. The house is steeply raked, so the sight lines are excellent. Even when there's nothing happening onstage, people can pass through the space and admire its gleaming glass walls with water views. Choreographers, musicians, and mixed media performers choose whether they want the glass to stay as is, for an instant aquatic backdrop, have the stage dimmed for a Turneresque blur, or have it completely blacked out. The ICA trustees decided to have a stage large enough for performances by companies the size of Mark Morris's and to have an expensive sprung floor. This meant that they'd never be in the position of retrofitting after cutting costs in round one in order to open on time, a situation Boston Ballet is in with its Grand Studio, which lacks appropriate seating.

The ICA, Wilder says, "is a wonderful story. It's venue as destiny. You ramp up the organization when you have a building. By not having a performance space of our own, people lose touch with us." While she notes that there will be another capital campaign in the future, she doesn't say when or what the money will be for.

The ICA's enviable situation emphasizes the difficult financial situation of ballet. Boston Ballet does have its own studio building at 19 Clarendon Street in Boston's South End, once a ramshackle, even dangerous neighborhood of brick row houses, now among the trendiest areas in the city, filled with chic restaurants, shops, and high-priced condos. The company moved into its new quarters, on the site of the former dingy garage where it used to rehearse, in 1991. The five-story building, by local architect Graham Gund, is fanciful, almost like a ballet set, with windows in varying shapes and sizes and little "Romeo and Juliet" balconies popping from the walls both indoors and out. It contains a large, function-worthy atrium, with administrative offices and seven studios for classes and rehearsals.

The building does not, however, house even a small theater where the company could give chamber-sized performances. The Grand Studio, the largest one, taking up much of the fourth floor with a high ceiling extending to the top of the building, would be an almost ideal space for small-scale performances, but as of late 2008 it didn't have permanent bleachers that would fold out of the wall for such events. The company couldn't afford them, and even in their closed position they would reduce the studio size by 12 feet. So, with some exceptions when risers have been rented, chairs are brought in and lined up at floor level, which means that the only full view of the dancing is from the front row.

Even if the Grand Studio had been better planned, or the building had included a performance space like that in the ICA, it couldn't accommodate, say, a full-length *Swan Lake* or other major works from the classical repertory.

When Wilder says that "the performing arts in America now are in a scary, nail-biting situation," she has foremost in mind the particularly precarious position of a ballet company without a suitable performance home. She adds, "It's not a field for the weak of heart. The ballet's $8 million deficit makes us extremely fragile. The end result will depend on how much this community wants to have a first-rate company, and now there's no question that we are first-rate. Boston is lucky to have a ballet company at all. The miracle is that we're still here."

After relations with the Wang came to a bitter end, in March 2008 Boston Ballet happily announced that it had struck a thirty-year deal with the Opera House, a 1928 vaudeville theater in downtown Boston. As of the 2009–10 season the facility would be the company's home—a smaller home for a smaller company, a more "intimate" experience, as Nissinen put it.

Also, after the news broke, Nissinen noted that the company sold more than 2,500 seats for a single performance only 5 percent of the time, so the 3,600 seats in the Wang weren't necessary, and the Opera House, at 2,580 seats, would be a good fit. What wouldn't be a good fit was the size of the Opera House stage. The dimensions say it all. The Opera House's width is 50' as opposed to the Wang's 60'3". The comparative depth is the real issue: the Opera House's depth is just under 43'; the Wang's is just over 76'.

Like the Wang, the Opera House presents Broadway shows and concerts. After the Ballet signed the new contract, Nissinen said that its particulars—what guarantee he had that some ballet program wouldn't be replaced by a rock show—were not something he could comment on, but he said he was comfortable with the agreement.

What Boston needs is a real opera house, built from the ground up, designed to meet the needs not only of Boston Ballet and the Boston Lyric Opera but also of visiting touring companies in both art forms. For want of a suitable venue, Boston has been off the touring circuit for such troupes. The city did have a proper opera house, but it was torn down in 1958 to make room for a dormitory for Northeastern University. Nissinen estimates that it would cost upwards of $150 million to build a new one.

Financial Support

A comparison of Boston Ballet's finances with those of other Boston arts mainstays helps to explain its perilous monetary status.

Gifts: Both the Boston Symphony Orchestra and the Museum of Fine Arts have been the recipients of eight-figure gifts. The MFA has four donors at what it calls the "Guardian" level, representing lifetime gifts of over $25 million. One of Boston Ballet's largest long-term donations has come from the family of former board chairman John Humphrey, whose contributions over the years have totaled close to $5 million. Boston Ballet's largest single gift was a $3.5 bequest from Dr. Beatrice Barrett, a local child psychiatrist who was a ballet aficionado. In 2008 there was a $2.5 million gift from a long-time board member, in addition to two $1 million gifts.

Campaigns: In the spring of 2008, the MFA announced it had raised $445 million toward its $500 million campaign to enlarge and refurbish its building. By comparison, Boston Ballet's campaign, which raised just over $36 million, was modest indeed.

Boston Ballet's endowment was $9 million by the spring of 2008, double what it was when Wilder arrived but tiny by the standards of other major companies. In the same year, New York City Ballet's endowment was around $180 million, San Francisco's was $75 million, and Houston's was $56 million.

"Our expenses rise and our revenues can't keep up" was Wilder's summary of the company's plight. The operating budget when she arrived at Boston Ballet was roughly $20 million. By the time she left in 2008, it had inched up to $24 million.

Nissinen's main complaint about Boston as a city is the lack of support from the public. "I find it extremely disappointing," he says. He's gotten almost unanimous praise for a dramatic upgrade in both the company's dancing and its repertory. But, he says, "the commitment isn't there financially." Wilder agrees. "Other arts organizations in Boston are getting funded." In addition to the big players, the MFA and the BSO, the university theaters—the American Repertory Theatre at Harvard and the Huntington Theatre at Boston University—get support from those educational institutions.

By the close of the spring 2007 season, the director of development was gone. So was the director of public relations. "We've seen a lot of unnecessary overlap among those departments and with marketing," Wilder said. "They're all trying to sell tickets and get donations." An almost comical case is a random telemarketing call to one of the Boston area's wealthiest citizens, with a request for $2,000. He wrote the check and considered himself off the solicitation hook until administrators higher up in the Ballet's organization successfully pressed him for more. Some sort of change was in order.

4

The Board of Trustees

It's the job of the Ballet's board of trustees to ensure that the company's continued presence in Boston is not a miracle but a given. It has been struggling to meet that goal since the company's founding.

Why do people want to sit on the boards of cultural institutions? For some, it's prestige, another rung up on the social ladder. For others, it's part of stepping up the corporate ladder: many large companies expect their executives to play a visible role in their communities, and serving on the board of an arts organization is one of the more pleasant ways of fulfilling that corporate duty. For others, and indeed for some of the corporate participants, it comes from a genuine sense of civic duty. Then there are those board members who are deeply interested in the art form.

In Boston, it is far more prestigious to sit on the board of the Museum of Fine Arts or the Boston Symphony Orchestra, both founded in the late nineteenth century by Boston Brahmins, than it is to sit on the board of a relative newcomer like Boston Ballet. E. Virginia Williams was advised by outside consultants to "get a Cabot on your board" (as in the ditty "And this is good old Boston / the home of the bean and the cod / where the Lowells talk only to Cabots / and the Cabots talk only to God"). Boston Ballet did snare a Cabot, but Maryellen Cabot and the board members she had brought with her left in protest after the 1984 resignation of artistic director Violette Verdy. Verdy and the Ballet's administration simply couldn't get along.

Even with a Cabot, the Ballet's board members have never been the kind of *Who's Who* of Boston society who sit on the BSO or MFA boards, nor do Ballet board members typically give the kind of money expected of BSO or MFA board members. The board spent much of 2007 whacking away at a budget that was already modest compared with those of other top U.S. companies.

Boston Ballet music director Jonathan McPhee has a skeptical view of boards of arts organizations. "They often think they know more than they do," he says. "They constantly have to have things explained to them to understand the operation." McPhee cited the New England Conservatory as a positive example of a board in Boston that was transformed through dynamic leadership. The late Daniel Steiner, after a career as general counsel of Harvard University, was the Conservatory's board chairman and then its president.

Steiner "professionalized the board, bringing in new people. Their predecessors couldn't have attracted the same people," says former *Boston Globe* classical music critic Richard Dyer. "The new people are experts in making money who also love, and know about, music." Steiner ran a $100 million campaign earmarked for scholarships and faculty salaries, so that the Conservatory could compete with Juilliard, Indiana University, and other top-notch music schools, luring faculty, especially string faculty, with high salaries. "They made themselves a major presence in the string world," Dyer says.

Boston Ballet's trustees must give or "get" (raise from others) $10,000 a year, Valerie Wilder said in 2007. "But some board members have really stepped up. The reputation of the Boston Ballet board as stagnant and insular is no longer correct." On leaving her job a year later, though, she noted the board's failure to present the company's case effectively enough to Boston's financial and civic leaders.

If the board had been stagnant, a set of term limits adopted in 2004 and finally implemented in late 2007 was intended to prevent that in the future. Before the new rules were put into effect, there were board members who had served for decades. Now they're on for three years, have to take a year off, and may then rejoin for another three-year term.

Jill Goldweitz, who had been on the board since the mid-1980s, was about to leave it at the end of 2007 because of the newly implemented term limits. For a time, she had been one of several Boston Ballet trustees who had served simultaneously on the boards of the Ballet and the Wang, which was more than ever a conflict of interest during the *Nutcracker* debacle when the Wang evicted the Ballet in order to book the Radio City Music Hall Christmas show. Because of a reconfigured board at the Wang and the prospect of one at the Ballet, there was no overlap as of the end of 2007.

Goldweitz laments that Boston Ballet has lost what she calls its "personality." In a nostalgic frame of mind, she recalls the days when she was bringing up her children in Boston's South End, near the company's building and would walk to the Ballet to serve as a full-time volunteer. "I feel as if I've grown up with the organization," she says. "It was my second home. As the company was growing up, we had dancers who were individuals." She mentions, as examples, former principals Laura Young, Elaine Bauer, and Donn Edwards. "The Ballet's strength was in them," she says. Now she acknowledges that "Mikko has done an absolutely brilliant job, although the company doesn't feel like a family anymore. It feels more professional, more unified in the dancing, without the principals who stood out. But it was time for Mikko to do what he did," which included a major housecleaning of staff and dancers after his 2001 arrival.

By the time the board hired Nissinen, it knew it wanted a director who knew something about management, the language most of them speak. So in the summer of 2002, with financial help from board chairman John Humphrey, Nissinen, whose formal education had never gone beyond high school courses, attended the Executive Program for Nonprofit Leaders in the Arts at Stanford University's Graduate School of Business.

Humphrey was cofounder, chairman, and CEO of The Forum Corporation, "which helped clients develop learning strategies and solutions and deploy their brands," according to the biography on his Web site. After Forum was sold, he became chairman and principal of Humphrey Enterprises LLC, a private equity investment firm. He had moved to Boston in 1981. "I fell in love with the city," he says. He and his family live in an elegant nineteenth-century brownstone on Commonwealth Avenue, one of the city's most sophisticated addresses. "I don't think there's a better place to live now," he says.

How did he choose which boards to be on? He purposefully picked the Franklin Park Zoo and Boston Ballet. Realistically, as a newcomer and an outsider, he knew he wouldn't make it onto the Boston Symphony Orchestra board. Besides, "The zoo needed a lot of help at that time. And the BSO didn't need me."

Pamela, his future wife, "had an interest in ballet, and I had an interest in Pam," he says. "It became apparent to me that many people think that a not-for-profit is supposed to be self-sufficient, but I fell in love with that whole philanthropic mode. I can't figure out why the Ballet doesn't draw a larger audience."

Humphrey served as chairman of the Ballet board three times: 1982–87, 1990–97, and 2000–2005. He worked with three directors or teams: Bruce Marks, Anna-Marie Holmes, and then Nissinen and Wilder. "I fired Anna-Marie," he says bluntly. "She couldn't manage the situation. I came back to the board chairmanship to hire Mikko and Valerie."

"We're evaluating what to do about the Wang," he said in 2007, before the permanent move to the Opera House was announced. The Wang "is the most expensive theater in the country. After we were thrown out for *Nutcracker,* we decided to keep a low profile, not to create a public fight between two nonprofits. We voted to stay at the Wang for performances other than *Nutcracker.* I didn't argue for or against it." Humphrey characterizes the instincts of Wang head Josiah Spaulding as "commercial. But there are performing arts centers all over the country that do commercial things."

Humphrey jokes that, in the manner of sports teams that very publicly advertise their sponsors, "we should have a little sign behind Giselle's grave that flashes 'Citizens Bank' on and off."

But distressing as the Ballet's situation may be, "I'm very optimistic about the company here. We scored big with Mikko. He's at the top of his game." Yet, in 2007, anticipating the drastic cuts to come, Humphrey asked, "Does Boston Ballet really need to do *Swan Lake*?" knowing that the cuts would leave a bare minimum number of dancers to produce that classic and others in a credible way.

Richard Davis, head of the Boston office of BlackRock, a New York–based investment management firm, is, like Humphrey, a relative newcomer to Boston. He moved to the area in 2001, after living in a New York City suburb. He says that he didn't often attend New York's ballet performances because it would have meant staying in town too late at night to see his children before their bedtime. He joined the Boston Ballet's board in 2001 and became its chairman in 2005. "I wanted to serve on a cultural board to become engaged with the community," he says. "I wanted a board where I could fit in and make a difference in an institution that wasn't already well established, like the BSO or MFA. I'd thought of joining a medical board, but they were all set, too.

"Corporate sponsorship for cultural institutions is down here and elsewhere," Davis says. "Civic responsibility is down. Corporations that have subsidiary offices here or elsewhere generally give where their headquarters are.

"I'm disappointed that the Ballet has such short seasons and such large gaps between programs," he adds. "We're missing an opportunity to grow through word of mouth." Neither he, Humphrey, nor Goldweitz expresses a vision for the company, other than Davis's thought that "if someone announced that Boston Ballet was folding, it might scare people into action."

A Boston Ballet trustee who grew up in the ballet world and then switched to the fashion retailing business—in other words, one whose résumé seems ideal for the board at Boston Ballet—is Eve Rounds, who is chair of the Ballet's overseers as well as a member of the board. "I grew up in New York and went to the School of American Ballet," she says. "I was there when Balanchine was still alive, and I was lucky enough to perform in his productions. He loved using children. *Coppelia* was one of the ballets he put me in." Many of the people Rounds met at SAB were legends. Her teachers included Alexandra Danilova and Felia Doubrovska. She had costume fittings with the great designer Karinska. "One day," Rounds recalls, "I went for a fitting, and my hair wasn't done up properly, and she screamed at me. I was 9 years old at the time."

She recalls, "In my family it was not an option not to go to college. So I left SAB for academics. I went to Smith College because they had a phenomenal dance program. We had a little troupe that traveled around. Then I transferred to Stanford where I did shows like *Cabaret.* Then I went into fashion retail. After I moved to Boston with my husband and sons, I also started taking classes at Boston Ballet. It seemed to me an obvious fit to enter the world of Boston Ballet, but fifteen years ago the company seemed kind of a closed group." After meeting a couple of the movers and shakers who were on Boston's board, she became an overseer and then a trustee.

The ever energetic Rounds and Margot Parsons, another Boston area balletomane and teacher, started "Dance on the Top Floor" to make use of Boston Ballet's Grand Studio for new works. "The goal," Rounds says, "was to showcase works by fledgling choreographers. After seven years, we took a breather. We were frustrated by not having publicity on what we were doing." Her goal of presenting new works mirrors Nissinen's, just as the lack of publicity for "Dance on the Top Floor" echoes Nissinen's frustration at half-empty houses.

Among her projects for Boston Ballet is sponsoring soloist Misa Kuranaga. "When she needs money for pointe shoes or to travel, I fund it," Rounds says. But her initiatives on behalf of the Ballet go far beyond sponsoring one dancer. Knowing full well how much the company required new blood on the board, she began a series of programs and events that were designed to give the board a transfusion by giving some training to current members and outsiders who were eligible.

"I started a Benefactor Program to actively cultivate potential donors through a series of cocktail events," she says. "The minimum gift is $2,000. We target both our friends and corporate groups. They watch rehearsals of what's about to play at the Wang, and then there's a Q&A with the dancers, all very informal. People in the Benefactors' Program have a chance to graduate to being an overseer, which will cost them a minimum donation of $5,000."

Another of Rounds's programs is "Lunch and Learn," held in the middle of the day. (Think of it as a ballet-based Rotary Club meeting.) "We invite all the overseers, board members, and their guests. An overseer pays for the lunch, and whoever that overseer is gets to decide the topic. One subject in the 2007–08 season will be the costume shop, because two overseers are involved in it as volunteers. This year we also had an overseer telephone every new subscriber to thank them. We didn't ask for money; we just called. The cultivation is important." (The word *cultivation* is heard in the administrative side of the Ballet as often as *plié* is heard on the artistic side.)

Overseers and trustees are at one end of the economic scale. Yet another of Rounds's projects, called "Ballet in the Balcony," is at the other. "They usually close off the Wang balcony—with its 1,500+ seats—because it's so far away from the stage," she says. "We thought, if the balcony is available, why not try to use it? We invited all Brookline high school students, their friends, and their families to regular performances. The tickets were $10 each. The rule the Ballet laid down was that because the Wang would charge us for rent and for the ushers, we had to have a minimum of 30 attendees to offset those expenses. We got an attendance of 700. Then I broadened the program to include the middle schools in Brookline. I picked Balanchine's *A Midsummer Night's Dream,* because every seventh-grader in Brookline has to read the play. We've now added other school systems to the program." So successful have Rounds's efforts been that SAB, where she trained long ago and where she is still involved with the advisory board, called on her to speak about how to get people into the theater.

Yet the local media haven't written much about her efforts to get teachers and students to come to the Ballet. "I thought this was a great subject for *The Tab,*" she says. *The Tab* is a chain of twelve weekly newspapers that land, free of charge, on the doorsteps of people living in Boston and its suburbs. "But I couldn't get an article about it," says Rounds. "I was flabbergasted. I even had a ballet parent call *The Tab,* and she couldn't convince them to write an article either."

Rounds's comment that ballet is a fragile art in a world that values tangibility is the crux of the problem of lack of support. "I'm passionate about Boston Ballet, about its survival and growth. But I think many of the staff and trustees there are all working on their own things. To be New York City Ballet and have an endowment that you can tap into if needed, that's great. But at Boston Ballet everyone is so focused on what they're doing at the moment. We have to connect the dots before things work. We're just scrambling."

5

The Choreographers

The Resident Choreographer

New York City Ballet, American Ballet Theatre, San Francisco Ballet, and Hubbard Street Dance Chicago are among the companies for which Jorma Elo has choreographed since Nissinen launched his career in the United States in 2002. Elo has also created pieces for European dance companies, including the Royal Danish Ballet. He's in demand, as announced on the cover of the April 2007 *Dance* magazine, with a headline that reads "Jorma Elo—Here There & Everywhere." The photographs accompanying that article give an indication of Elo's style. On the cover he crouches close to the ground, with feet turned in, one leg straight and the other bent, fingers splayed, and torso leaning back and listing sideways. It's hard to tell whether his position is aggressive or defensive. He looks like some exotic animal about to rally its forces and pounce on its prey. On the other hand, he looks a bit like Odette, the Swan Queen, in the second act of *Swan Lake,* protecting herself with her bent arms and wrists, also with one leg straight and the other bent.

However odd his pose, Elo's choreography is completely rooted in classical ballet. Born in Helsinki in 1961, he spent most of his career performing with European companies: seven years with Finnish National Ballet, seven with Sweden's Cullberg Ballet, and fourteen with Nederlands Dans Theater. During his time with NDT he started choreographing, and in 1999 his childhood friend, Mikko Nissinen, invited him to create two works for Alberta Ballet in Canada, which Nissinen was then directing. After Nissinen became artistic director of Boston

Jorma Elo watching a rehearsal of his version of *Carmen* at the Citi Performing Arts Center Wang Theatre. Photo by Wally Gilbert.

Ballet in 2001, he brought Elo along with him, appointing him resident choreographer in 2002.

Elo, who is on a salary with the company and whose contract ran through 2009 but was renewed in 2008 through 2014, has made one work a year for Boston, and they've all been well received—except for his only foray into a story ballet, his *Carmen,* which met with resoundingly negative reviews from Boston critics. (I liked it, but only after watching it three times.)

While I had seen all the works Elo had done for Boston and watched his rehearsals, I hadn't had the chance to interview him. So I spent a week with him in Copenhagen in August 2007, watching him rehearse with the Royal Danish Ballet. I had been told by Elizabeth Olds, Nissinen's assistant and Elo's representative, that while both Nissinen and Elo are Finns, they have entirely different personalities. Nissinen is gregarious and outgoing, essential qualities these days for artistic directors, who must spend a considerable chunk of their time looking rich people in the eye, smiling, asking them about their kids, and then assessing how to ask them for money. It's not the stereotype of a Finn.

On the first day of watching rehearsals in Copenhagen, I tried to break the ice by noting that Elo was wearing Adidas workout clothes. "Is Adidas your corporate sponsor?" I asked. He grinned and said, "Yes. Every month they send me lots of money and say, 'Thank you, Mr. Elo.'" Like most dancers in this post-Baryshnikov age, when there are no more superstars who can command enormous fees, he is frustrated by the lack of funds in his field and by the lack of attention paid to it.

Early in his life he did want to be a sports star, someone who actually would get paid for wearing a particular brand of clothing. "I was into hockey," he says, "which is very big in Finland. When I was 10 or 11, I wanted to be a pro hockey player." The vestiges of his athletic ambitions survive in his tennis: no matter where he is, he tries to play every day. He came from a medical family, including a doctor, dentist, and nurse. "It was shocking to my parents to have their only son go the wrong way, not to go to university. My sisters studied modern dance—Graham and Cunningham—at a private school in Helsinki. The school gave me a scholarship. They also had ballet classes, and I tried them and found I loved expressing myself to music. I thought, 'This is even better than hockey.'"

At age 13 he enrolled in the Finnish National Ballet School, where he met Nissinen, who was a year younger. The Helsinki school offered only ballet training. Ballet classes were after real school. "We went to 'normal' school," Elo says, "and at 4 p.m. we would run for the bus to go to ballet lessons. Sometimes we would skip school in the mornings to watch the professional dancers' class.

"Mikko and I joined Finnish National Ballet when I was 16 and Mikko was 15. After two years with the company, we got scholarships to go to Leningrad, to the Kirov school. We'd seen all these books on Nureyev, Solovyov, and the other great dancers who came out of that school. We had also seen American Ballet Theatre in Copenhagen, with Mikhail Baryshnikov and Gelsey Kirkland dancing and Twyla Tharp's *Push Comes to Shove*. We just wanted to go to the school that had produced Baryshnikov.

"Mikko got a scholarship to the Kirov School right away because of his virtuosity. I got a place because somebody else dropped out," he says. That's Finnish modesty kicking in. "I didn't feel that I got the best coaching in Leningrad. I was disappointed in it. The teachers focused on a few students they felt had great talent. They were the ones who were nurtured. I didn't have that great technique that Mikko had. But to be on the Kirov stage was magic. Leningrad is a beautiful city, but it was also odd. It was like this big set for a film noir, with pastel palaces on the one hand and all the people wearing gray on the other.

"The winter there was very hard. There was nothing in the shops. Once a week something would arrive. I'd line up for an hour to get it and bring it back to the dorm room that Mikko and I shared with two guys from East Germany. Once a shop was selling raisins. I bought 20 years worth of raisins. I had to leave most of them behind when Mikko and I left the Soviet Union."

After a few more years in Finland, Elo moved on to the Cullberg Ballet, which was directed by Mats Ek, whose mother, Birgit Cullberg, had founded the troupe. "I wanted to experiment more," Elo says. "I knew what my future would be in Finland. Maybe I could be a demi-soloist and do the pas de trois in *Swan Lake,* but it wouldn't be anything more." Ek's ideas about choreography—the second act of his *Giselle* is set in an insane asylum, because Giselle does, after all, go mad—"opened my eyes to a whole new way of making dances, of thinking about choreography. It was a great company, and Mats was very inspiring as a dancer/actor/coach.

"Then I went to NDT, and it was so overwhelmingly creative. They would have these workshops for dancers with twenty people doing choreography. Plus there would be Mats Ek, Ohad Naharin [an Israeli choreographer], and Jiři Kylián [then the artistic director of NDT], all making new works for the company. The atmosphere was all about making dances. You had to be pulled into that stream or else leave. You had to create. I got drawn into it." Elo says that Kylián didn't teach choreography, nor was he a hands-on mentor. He set an example with his own work, and then put everybody else into the studios and let them make dances. "The workshops didn't have to result in masterpieces as long as people were thinking and moving."

Elo was 43 when he left the company in 2004. "That's when I stopped dancing. I was lucky that my body lasted that long. By that time, if I had one ballet to dance a night instead of three, I was happy. I was already choreographing for Alberta Ballet, Finnish National Ballet, and NDT. It was a good transition. As a dancer at the end of my career, I tried to be tuned into the moment, to notice what the humidity was like in the studio, what the room was like, not to look back, but to make everything new." He compares this to "a musician who takes that one beautiful note and makes it seem new, although he's been practicing it for thirty years."

Alberta and Nissinen were key to Elo's continuing growth as a choreographer. "Mikko had several wonderful dancers there, including Sabi Varga," currently a Boston Ballet soloist. Varga is one of the regulars in Elo's works for Boston. In the few companies for which the choreographer has done more than one work, with Boston at the top of the list, he's tended to develop a company within the company, a group of dancers he's become accustomed to working with and whom he asks the artistic director for again when he returns. "It's often the case that you prefer to use the same dancers. You've made a connection with these people, and it's easier to go on from there."

In most ballet companies, including Boston's, choreographers come to stage a work, then travel to their next assignment and leave the ongoing rehearsal duties to a company ballet master who has sat in on the initial process and taken notes. A few months later, the choreographer shows up again for the second chapter in the rehearsal process, and sometimes there's a third or even fourth chapter as well, the last one generally taking place right before the first performance. Even though Elo is Boston Ballet's "resident" choreographer, he's in residence only while rehearsing a piece. Otherwise, he's shuttling between the United States and Europe. "I love to travel now, but maybe someday I won't," he says, mentioning the possibility of one day directing his own company. He and his companion/collaborator, Nancy Euverink, still have a house in The Hague, where NDT is headquartered, and when Elo comes to Boston, he's put up in a hotel. He's not picky about hotels, which is a good thing, because some companies have billeted him in quite modest ones. "Sometimes the hotel rooms in Paris are really tiny. But I wouldn't stay in a five-star hotel with a gourmet restaurant even if I could afford it," he says. "You have to dress up and wear a tie and wait a long time for your food." I've never seen Elo in anything but workout wear and T-shirts.

Elo videotapes every minute of every rehearsal. He leaves one copy of the tape with the ballet master and dancers and keeps another for himself, to watch while he's on the road. A considerable chunk of the rehearsal time in whatever country he's in is spent with the dancers huddled around a TV monitor or laptop. They watch what happened a few months earlier and go from there. The obsessive recording is also necessary because Elo is so prolific that he doesn't remember every dance he's made. "With some choreographers, the ballets are like their babies. They carry them around constantly. I don't do that." Sounding like he's running a choreographic adoption agency, he says, "For me, it's the dancers who hold onto the babies."

The dancers also sometimes contribute to the dance. In Copenhagen, one woman half-jokingly interjected the signature jump from August Bournonville's *La Sylphide*—legs low and behind, back arched, curving arms extending the arc of the legs—and Elo says, "Yes, let's do that. Bournonville is in the air here. I can't deny it." So this small echo of Bournonville turns up in the dance.

In rehearsal Elo can't seem to stand still. While demonstrating complicated lifts with Euverink, who once danced with Boston Ballet II and is also a former NDT dancer, there seemed nothing that the two of them couldn't do and no shape they couldn't achieve. He swung her overhead with the ease of a cowboy expertly wielding a lariat. No matter how novel his gestures, though, his ballet background shows. Watching the dancers, with his back to the barre in the studio, he performed a series of changements, jumps where the feet trade places, ending in a perfectly crossed fifth position. Despite stopping his performing career a few years ago, he's in great shape. Wherever he is, he takes company class every day.

In addition to demonstrating physically, both Elo and Euverink are also good at coaching the dancers verbally, often with metaphor. When he wants the Danes to drop their heads quickly and then recover, she says, "It's like what happens when you get sleepy sitting on a bus." The rhythm and dynamic of the gesture are instantly clear.

Elo's method of working with dancers is almost like a meditation session. He'll go up to an individual dancer to make a point and speak so quietly that it's almost a whisper. The other dancers would have to come quite near to hear it. When he's speaking to several dancers at once, it's equally calm, although there are occasional bouts of laughter. He is utterly focused and quiet, and that manner is contagious. Even when dancers are flying through the air, they have a sense of composure.

Choreography, for Elo, is a slow process. "I start with the music," he says. "I listen to it over and over. I think of solutions I've made before and how I can evolve from there and make it more interesting for my eye and also be surprised by it." While he familiarizes himself with the music, he doesn't ask the dancers to listen to it outside the studio, and in an hourlong rehearsal he may turn on the taped score for only a few minutes. He likes to watch how the dancers perform the movement he gives them without having the music dictate when they do what. (He's the opposite of Mark Morris, who so reveres the music that he leads rehearsals with the score in his hand, sometimes humming and gesturing with one arm as if he were conducting.)

Does Elo think of the dancers as conducting the music? "That's a good way to put it," he says. While in rehearsal, at least in the initial stages, it doesn't matter to him whether they're in unison. By the time of the premiere they will be, if that's what he's decided the choreography calls for.

His titles are usually enigmatic. *Sharp Side of Dark, Plan to B,* and *Brake the Eyes* are the names of pieces he's done for Boston. (He's done a *Carmen* as well, but you don't have much leeway with names when you're choreographing to the iconic Bizet score.) The names take a long time gestating. "People are always coming up to me at the last minute, when the program has to be printed, and asking for the title," he says. How does he come up with it? "I start with the work itself. I look at it and think, 'This is something sharp, and this is something dark.' I just make a long list and get words that are visually pleasing to me."

In late 2007 he was in Boston for a few weeks to work on another new piece for the company. No, it didn't yet have a name. But it had a very specific inspiration: Bernard Herrmann's score for Alfred Hitchcock's *Vertigo.* Elo was going through a Hitchcock phase, with another work percolating for the Royal Ballet of Flanders, set to music from Hitchcock's *North by Northwest,* also by Herrmann, who was one of the great film composers of the twentieth century, with the score to Orson Welles's *Citizen Kane* also to his credit.

In his new work for Boston, Elo would ultimately splice in other music besides the score for *Vertigo,* to create the sort of sound environment he likes working with. His combinations of sounds drive to distraction Boston Ballet's music director, Jonathan McPhee, who is more accustomed to working traditionally, conducting a ballet from start to finish as the composer wrote it. Elo is the opposite, deconstructing and then reassembling scores.

The black and white of Hitchcock's films "make them sort of spooky,"

Elo says. But in the new piece for Boston, "Everything will be blue and green, even the floor. I wasn't thinking of water, just a vertiginous wall that closes in on you. It's like Chinese water torture, one drop at a time on you." These last remarks do suggest Hitchcock and *Vertigo.* The movements that the Boston dancers were practicing most, shimmering fingers and liquid torsos among them, bore less direct relation to the film.

In rehearsal one woman was using her hands as if they were holding puppet strings attached to her leg, which levitated obediently. Other dancers' heads were wiggling independently as if they were about to topple off their necks.

This sort of fragmentation of the body is one of Elo's trademarks. The vocabulary of traditional ballet calls for graceful if formulaic gestures in which heads, shoulders, and arms respond harmoniously to legs and feet. None of that for him. The piece would, however, retain some of the elegant bravura for which Elo is also known.

The new Boston piece would have a cast of three women and nine men with, especially for Elo, a rather conventional relationship among them. "I thought I would bring out three really extraordinary creatures, fragile, like sylphs," he says. The work wouldn't be danced for another five months, but already he had chosen his first cast, with Larissa Ponomarenko, Erica Cornejo, and Melissa Hough as the three women. They'll look airborne, but "they won't really have to be unless I can pay off Mikko's deficit, plus the cost of flying. Then I'll do it."

"The nine guys," he says, "will be masculine, with raw energy, an earthy contrast to the fragility of the women." One gesture he has Sabi Varga practice is a slide across the floor that resembles a baseball player sliding into a base. Elo demonstrates it. Varga follows, not getting as far. "But, mister, you've got socks on" is Varga's rationale for Elo's outdoing him.

Elo admits to not having much of a business sense. "Mikko owns the rights to the ballets I've done for him," he says. "But I don't even know for how many years and what the contract says. Mikko has given me this wonderful opportunity. Anything I can do for Boston Ballet, I will." Which included being in Boston for the March 6, 2008, premiere of his latest work for the company, the day before his premiere for the Royal Danish Ballet. Timing and flight schedules would prevent him from attending both premieres.

Elo, who commutes between Europe and the United States, makes it sound as if choreography is a religious calling, a monkish lifestyle. He doesn't *want* an expensive one. He wants to make dances. In the summer of 2007 he found himself with a six-week gap in his schedule. Quite atypically, he filled the time with a cruise, a visit to Greece, and a visit with his family. "Holidays make me nervous. But what is 'work' for other people isn't for me. It's just what I want to do. Besides," he says, sounding like the true solitary Scandinavian, "on holiday you have to mingle with other people."

The Fledgling Choreographer

"I want to be a graceful, generous person," Helen Pickett says, "to lead a graceful life. I don't know if I do, but that's the goal." Both she and Elo are modest people, focused on their work. (Balanchine had a similar attitude. There are photographs of him ironing shirts, and when Kirstein once encouraged him to visit the Metropolitan Museum of Art, his response was "I've already been there.")

Born in San Diego in 1967, Pickett has had about as varied a dance career as anyone could imagine. She studied at the San Francisco Ballet's school. The brothers Christensen—Lew, William, and Harold—were still alive. The three had pioneered ballet in the West with San Francisco Ballet, the oldest classical company in the country.

"Lew was still teaching company class, and the doors were always open," says Pickett. "You know how young dancers are so enamored of the whole glamour of ballet. Even as a child you understand that an older person is part of the history of the dance world." Her teacher was Anatole Vilzak, whose pedigree went all the way back to Diaghilev's Ballets Russes.

"The children in the San Francisco Ballet school performed in *Nutcracker,* but I also did the Hounds in *Midsummer Night's Dream,*" she says proudly. "It seemed that when we were picked, I ended up doing animals. I was a dog and a chicken, but I also did corps roles. I was never in the actual company, though. When Billy Forsythe came to San Francisco Ballet to stage his *New Sleep,* I sat in the doorway day after day, watching. He's like a magician who knows how to draw things out of the dancers. I ended up in the piece. Billy said he would give me a contract."

Helen Pickett with students at Boston Ballet's Summer Dance Program. Photo by Wally Gilbert.

SFB artistic director Helgi Tomasson "called me into the office and offered me an apprenticeship contract if I stayed," she recalls. "But I'd been to Frankfurt, and I'd already fallen in love with Europe. It was the best decision I ever made. My whole life changed because of it."

Frankfurt Ballet's experimental approach was a far cry from San Francisco's relative conservatism. "We would write some of our own text for speaking parts," Pickett recalls. "I interviewed other dancers for a film. We sang. It was so broad. Billy said, 'This is what dance can turn into, a well-rounded art form.' We had to read a lot, too. I remember reading about the architect Daniel Libeskind for one piece."

Then she developed knee problems. "The first time I blew out my kneecap, Billy just popped it back in. The second time, I had reconstructive surgery. My surgeon was a magician. I could take class. I could jog. I retired from Frankfurt in 1998, after eleven years. Leaving Billy was the hardest decision I ever made."

As with other famous choreographers—the prime example being Martha Graham, whose company's rights to perform her works were confirmed only following a bitter legal battle after her death—Pickett says, "Billy knows the people who say they're teaching his technique. And he knows the bogus ones. I say I teach a Forsythe-based improvisation technique. When I run into people saying they teach the Forsythe Technique, I ask them, 'When were you in the company?' I feel that's my duty to him. He wants that integrity kept up."

After leaving Forsythe, Pickett performed in what's generally called "alternative media," a combination of acting, filmmaking, singing, speaking, and other art forms—until she taught what turned out to be a fateful improvisation workshop for MIT, held in the studios of Boston Ballet. One day, she boldly went upstairs to Nissinen's office, knocked on the door, and asked him if he wanted to watch her improvise. He did.

After she had left Boston and that improv class, Nissinen called her and asked if she would be interested in making a work for Boston Ballet. "I'd already convinced myself that I didn't want to choreograph, but within an hour after I hung up, I was shaking, and all the ideas came to me. It was a fear response. I'd known Mikko since 1986, when I took class in Basel, then when he was in San Francisco Ballet. We hadn't kept in touch. In this country, though, and also as a woman, you have to learn the intricacies of getting yourself out there." Other than Bronislava Nijinska, in the twentieth century there were few great women choreographers whose work was exclusively in the classical dance idiom, which Nijinska, like her brother Vaslav, and like her contemporary George Balanchine, helped to transform.

Both Pickett and Elo continue that transformation but, like Nijinska and Balanchine, remain rooted in the classical tradition. You see that in the easy rapport they have with the Boston dancers, a rapport that has not always been present in the studio when "modern" choreographers come to town. The tradition was inculcated in both Elo and Pickett by classical training in a superb company, and in each case it was modulated by years in a continental milieu. That such a combination has worked so well in Boston to date may reflect as much the standards that Nissinen has introduced there as it does the inherent quality of the European experience.

6

The Dancers

A Changing Company

Professional ballet dancers are both exquisite, almost superhuman creatures and at the same time normal young people. As the Boston Ballet's dancers try on costumes just before a rehearsal of the nineteenth-century ballet *Raymonda,* they talk about whether to have Thai take-out for dinner or go to Burger King, what time the Laundromat closes, and what time *The O.C.* is on television. The costumes they're wearing are a regal contrast to this patter. Made of white and gold satin adorned with faux pearls and diamonds, they suggest the attire of the medieval Hungarian court that is the setting for *Raymonda.*

Like a court, a ballet company has a hierarchy. Nissinen sees his troupe as a pyramid, with the corps dancers a solid base, the soloists the next rung up, and the principals like diamonds, shining at the top. Nissinen has in fact added a level to that hierarchy: there used to be corps, soloist, and principal dancers. Nissinen instituted two tiers of soloists. "I have this generation of very good dancers coming up," he says. "Another level of soloist is an incentive for them to want to progress from one rank to the next. The first soloists really stand out. They routinely land principal roles." Promotion from soloist to principal involves economic as well as artistic considerations, since a principal dancer's contract costs more than a soloist's.

Despite Nissinen's pride in his dancers, it could be argued that more than most artistic directors he sees the choreographers as the stars. He wants to bring as much attention as possible to those who have caught

Kathleen Breen Combes rehearsing Mark Morris's *Up and Down*. Photo by Wally Gilbert.

his eye, including Jorma Elo, Helen Pickett, and company soloist Heather Myers, a burgeoning talent Nissinen also wants to promote.

Promoting choreographers, though, isn't possible without dancers whose style the artistic director likes, and when Nissinen came to Boston Ballet he did not find them. Of the fifty dancers on the company's roster in 2007–08, only six were there when he arrived. He hired the rest himself, remaking the company to achieve the "look" and the spirit he wants.

Hiring dancers is fraught with political and psychological issues. One reason Nissinen brought in Lorna Feijóo in 2003 was to give Larissa Ponomarenko, considered the company's reigning ballerina at that point, some competition. The two make a stunning contrast the few times they are onstage together. Ponomarenko is a pale blonde wisp with a reticent manner; Feijóo is dark and expressive, eager to share her feelings with audiences.

At the end of the spring 2007 season, of the ten principal dancers on the roster five were from Spanish-speaking countries, verifying Lynn Garafola's 2004 *Dance* magazine article "Sweeping the Stage: Why Latin Is the New Russian." The most prominent were Feijóo and her husband, Nelson Madrigal, who joined the company after sitting out (and leaping and turning) a year with Cincinnati Ballet, because Nissinen didn't have two principal contracts when they arrived in the United States. Directors budget the number of principal, soloist, and corps contracts they will have available a year or two in advance of the actual season.

In 2007 Nissinen said that the 50 dancers then in the company, plus the 9 in Boston Ballet II, were the absolute "minimum" for producing a "big" ballet like *Swan Lake*. He mentions that, by contrast, the Bolshoi Ballet in Moscow has 220 dancers.

Then came the news that the company would be cut to 41 starting in the fall of 2009. It would be a smaller company in a smaller house. The company's spin was that it would make for a more "intimate" experience and that the dancers and audience would be closer together.

The dancers in the current company come from Japan, Australia, Hungary, Spain, Cuba, Russia, Bulgaria, Colombia, France, and a few other countries. This United Nations approach has a downside. True, Boston Ballet has now risen to a level that attracts dancers from all over the world. On the other hand, it means the Boston Ballet School isn't yet producing many dancers for the company, and that means that however talented the dancers Nissinen hires, they are not trained in quite the same style, so there is a lot of retraining going on.

As for the touchy matter of choosing dancers and casting them in ballets, "I have all the dancers in the company audition for every ballet, no matter if it's a corps dancer or a principal. A couple of years ago I had a principal who just didn't cut it. So he didn't get a part he expected to. I do most of the casting because I know the company better than anyone else. The exception is Mark Morris," Nissinen says. "I just let him have whoever he wants."

Artistic directors look for particular qualities when they choose dancers. They need dancers either tall or short for a particular production, ballerinas who can be relied on to do those thirty-two fouetté turns in the third act of *Swan Lake,* dancers who are good at experimenting with choreographers.

The use of dancers depends not only on their own talent but also on the choreography the director is planning for future seasons. Hence the fate of Jennifer Gelfand, a child prodigy brought up in Boston Ballet, a dancer who could do anything technically—including triple turns in the treacherous *Swan Lake* fouettés. But in 2003 she parted ways with the company where she had spent most of her working life. "Mikko has a vision of what he wants," she said at the time. When she announced her departure that spring, she said he had passed her over in casting decisions. "I wasn't going to stay around and be miserable trying to find out what he wants," she said. She was 31, an audience favorite, and could easily have danced much longer. But she had planned ahead years before by starting to sell real estate—she sold Nissinen his South End home—and she chose to do that full time.

Romi Beppu, a Hawaiian-born dancer who had joined the company in the corps in 1998 and become a soloist in 2003 and principal in 2005, resigned in the spring of 2008 to join Ballet West in Salt Lake City. Jorma Elo had not used her in any of the ballets he had done for Boston, and Elo was the choreographer Nissinen wanted to keep pushing, the one whose American career he had launched. When Boston Ballet revived Nissinen's *Swan Lake* in 2008, Beppu, who had previously danced the dual leading role as well as subsidiary parts, wasn't chosen for a major role. She saw Ballet West's offer as a welcome opportunity, in the short career of a dancer, to try new repertory in a new setting.

About to leave, she criticized some of Boston's past repertory, especially the two Ben Stevenson ballets, *Dracula* and *Cleopatra,* which involved sets and costumes that drowned the dancers and had very little in the way of anything resembling choreography. "I was wearing a blue wig and crawling on the floor in *Cleopatra.* After 10 years of training, I wondered why." On the other hand, Beppu says, "I love the contemporary repertory here. I've been in all of Helen Pickett's ballets. She lifts your spirits. At those 5:30 rehearsals, after a really long day, she'll start with a joke."

Ashley Blade-Martin and her husband, Alfonso Martin, left Boston Ballet after only one season, 2006–07. In Boston, they were both in the corps. Prior to that, they had spent several years with the Tulsa Ballet in Oklahoma, he as a principal and she as a soloist, ranks they resumed after their Boston experience. "We both helped build that company," Blade-Martin said of the Tulsa troupe. "We weren't used enough in Boston."

Sarah Lamb, who trained with Tatiana Legat at the Boston Ballet School, quickly rose through the ranks in the company she joined in 1998. In 2003 Nissinen promoted her to principal. That same year she bolted to join England's Royal Ballet, where she was a first soloist and then in short order became a principal in that company. On leaving Boston she complained bitterly and openly about Legat having been let go. (Nissinen says it was part of budgetary cuts.) "Madame Legat," Lamb says, "taught me that the fingertips, épaulement, and use of the arms are the voice, the punctuation, the nuances that must all emanate from the centre to express oneself" ("A Conversation with Sarah Lamb," October 28, 2005, <http://auguste.vestris.free.fr/Interviews/SarahLamb .html>). Lamb said that generally the subtlety that Legat taught her is missing in American ballet.

Nissinen put a positive spin on her defection: for Lamb to dance major roles with one of the most illustrious companies in the world reflects well, he says, on the company he's building in Boston.

There are a few Boston-bred dancers who have left the city under happier circumstances and gone on to glory. One is Damian Woetzel, who trained at the Boston Ballet School and went on to become a star with New York City Ballet. While still at City Ballet he earned a graduate degree in the Mid-Career Master in Public Administration Program at Harvard's Kennedy School of Government—a remarkable feat, since he had never gone to college.

Larissa Ponomarenko rehearsing with Francia Russell and Anthony Randazzo, in George Balanchine's *La Valse*, choreography by George Balanchine, © The George Balanchine Trust. Photo by Wally Gilbert.

Trinidad Vives
rehearsing
Raymonda, act 3.
Photo by Wally
Gilbert.

Jorma Elo speaking
to Jonathan McPhee
during a rehearsal
of *Carmen* at the
Citi Performing
Arts Center Wang
Theatre. Photo by
Wally Gilbert.

Karine Seneca in
The Dying Swan at
the Citi Perform-
ing Arts Center
Wang Theatre.
Photo by Wally
Gilbert.

Lorna Feijóo in class
with Luca Sbrizzi, Yury
Yanowsky, and Gabor
Kapin. Photo by Wally
Gilbert.

Christopher
Budzynski in
Gopak at the Citi
Performing Arts
Center Wang
Theatre. Photo by
Wally Gilbert.

Karine Seneca and
the company in
Les Noces at the
Citi Performing
Arts Center Wang
Theatre. Photo by
Wally Gilbert.

Christopher
Budzynski and
the company in
Les Noces at the
Citi Performing
Arts Center Wang
Theatre. Photo by
Wally Gilbert.

Misa Kuranaga
and Reyneris Reyes
rehearsing the
ribbon dance from
La Fille mal gardée.
Photo by Wally
Gilbert.

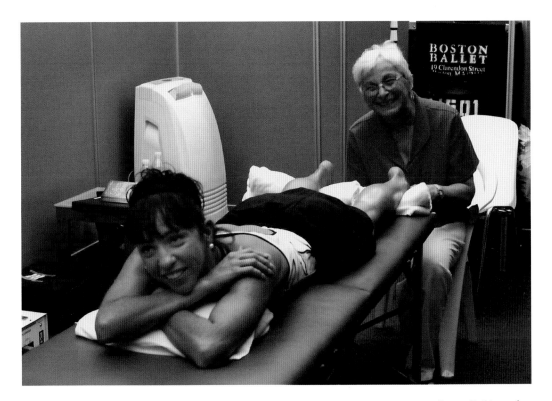

Lorna Feijóo and
Michelina Cassella
in physical therapy.
Photo by Wally
Gilbert.

Jared Redick and
Arthur Leeth
rehearsing *La Fille
mal gardée*. Photo
by Wally Gilbert.

Maina Gielgud
adjusting Tiffany
Hedman's hair for
a *Giselle* rehearsal.
Photo by Wally
Gilbert.

Larissa Ponoma-
renko and Roman
Rykine in rehearsal
for *Giselle*. Photo
by Wally Gilbert.

Mark Morris
rehearsing Brooke
Reynolds and
Bradley Schlagheck
for *Up and Down*.
Photo by Wally
Gilbert.

Mark Morris
choreographing *Up
and Down*. Photo
by Wally Gilbert.

Ashley Blade-Martin in a pause during a rehearsal. Photo by Wally Gilbert.

Larissa Ponomarenko

Larissa Ponomarenko, originally from Ukraine, trained at the Vaganova Ballet Academy in St. Petersburg, Russia, the feeder school for the Maryinsky Ballet Company, aka the Kirov. For many, the Vaganova Ballet Academy is ballet heaven. Ponomarenko later danced with the Donetsk Ballet Company in Ukraine, then as a guest artist in the United States with Tulsa Ballet Theatre and Ballet Mississippi. As fine as those organizations may be, they are hardly among the world's top classical troupes. Why, after training in the Soviet Union, didn't she try out for the Kirov or a U.S. company like American Ballet Theatre? She did. "I was accepted as a company member at the Kirov," she says. "But at the time it was the fashion to have taller dancers." She is 5'2¾". "My teacher told me that if I stayed in St. Petersburg, I'd only dance the parts for short girls, like the cygnets in *Swan Lake*."

Ponomarenko joined Boston Ballet as a principal in 1993, hired by Bruce Marks, and is one of the few company dancers to predate Nissinen's regime. For her, the hardest part of Nissinen's tenure has been "to see waves of people coming and going. There have been fantastic dancers who got discouraged and left. I'm a person who doesn't become friends easily with other people. I have high standards for relationships. Whenever I make a friend in the company, a girlfriend, she leaves. The plan is that when we're all 70, we'll retire together to Hawaii or the South of France. I wouldn't mind that at all.

"Once I joined Boston Ballet I had such great coaching that it never occurred to me to leave." The coaching came primarily from Tatiana Legat, heir to a great name in Russian dance. Her grandfather was Nicholas Legat, a famed teacher and coach at the Maryinsky in St. Petersburg, whose pupils included Nijinsky and Pavlova. "Madame Legat was a walking encyclopedia of dancing," Ponomarenko says. "She would look at a person's body and always set a higher bar. She was tough. She would make me cry sometimes. For a lot of people in the company it was difficult to work with her because she was so tough, so detailed in her coaching. But the only videos I like of myself are the ones coached by her."

Nissinen disagrees about Tatiana Legat. "I thought when I got here that Boston Ballet had only the Russian perspective and that there were other outlooks, other techniques. I think that many ballet syllabi are out of date. Ballet training has to be brought into the twenty-first century. I try to mix the best of the best."

Ponomarenko turned 37 in 2007. "By the time I thought of leaving Boston Ballet, it was already too late," she says sadly. A lateral move to a different but equally good company was unlikely. "I'm not a very good manager of my career. I have to remind myself that this is my work. I have to close my heart when I come to the studio and just do my professional bit." On a more positive note, "I've been lucky to dance the repertory I have in Boston." Her signature role is Tatiana in John Cranko's masterpiece *Onegin,* based on Alexander Pushkin's novel in verse. Cranko created the role on his main muse, Marcia Haydee, but he might as well have made it specifically for Ponomarenko, so perfectly suited was she to play the bookish ingénue who matures into a noble and tragic heroine.

One dancer who left Boston Ballet was her husband, Viktor Plotnikov, who was unhappy that Nissinen redefined his role from principal dancer to character artist, which meant acting roles, generally portraying older men or eccentrics, like the mysterious Drosselmeier in *Nutcracker,* or villains like Von Rothbart in *Swan Lake.* Now Plotnikov choreographs for companies in smaller cities around the United States. "I don't see him much," Ponamarenko says wistfully. "We used to see each other twenty-four hours a day. Now sometimes I don't see him for three weeks."

She now has to plan the second half of her working life. "The tendency in the United States when you stop dancing is to do something completely new. But I would like to stay in the field, working with young dancers, maybe staging some of Viktor's ballets." Ponomarenko has remained a stranger in a strange land, still writing down English words she doesn't understand, and then not having time to look them up, she says. But there's no going back. "My country now is a mess. I would be irrelevant there. Viktor and I return every year to visit our families. I miss the opportunity to perform for them."

Bo Busby

Nissinen was very proud of having six male dancers over 6' tall on the 2007–08 roster. Female dancers grow several inches when they go up on pointe. Partnering them is mechanically easier if the man is taller, or at

least equally tall, when the woman rises on toe. Aesthetica
nership also looks better than when the woman towers ove

Bo Busby, born in 1983 in Newberry, South Carolina,
tallest of the tall in Boston Ballet. In green practice wear
the Jolly Green Giant, whose signature "Ho, ho, ho" also
personality. His real name is Albert Foster Busby III, "but
the program," he says. "It's a cool stage name."

His mother was his first dance teacher. But as she beca
quit teaching ballet and took a job with Saks Fifth Avenue
earn more money and also get benefits. Dancers, except for those in a
union company like Boston's, don't necessarily have health insurance,
pensions, or other benefits that so many workers take for granted, nor
can dancers work until they're a "normal" retirement age. Pinned to the
wall in a Boston Ballet corridor at the end of 2007 was a sign advertis-
ing an in-house seminar on making transitions out of dancing when the
time comes. It's a not uncommon realization in ballet companies that
they owe their loyal dancers some guidance to their second roles in life
after using up their youths.

Busby is far from thinking of leaving dance. "I've been dancing since
I was 4, taking lessons with Mom," he says. "Instead of my running
around the house aimlessly wreaking havoc, I'd dress up as a superhero
and pretend to be someone else. I like being someone else." He makes a
surprising analogy that perhaps dates from his superhero phase: "Being
a dancer is like being a Navy SEAL. You get to blow stuff up." The dance
equivalent isn't violent, but as Busby defines the rush of being onstage
and then hearing applause and "Bravo!" there *is* a connection in the
thrill of the moment.

"Dressing up and playing different characters is fun. You're a prince
one day and Von Rothbart the next." The latter was a role he particularly itched to dance. "You're in full body makeup. You're all green!" He
finally had his chance in the spring 2007 season.

He was already in American Ballet Theatre, which is still generally
held in higher regard than Boston Ballet, when he came to Boston with
his girlfriend, Karen Uphoff, to visit her sister, Kimberly Uphoff, who
is in Boston Ballet's corps. He took class in Boston, and Nissinen offered him a job. That was in 2006. Why leave ABT? "I wanted to dance
more," he says. "I was too tall for many corps roles, the ones where the
guys all have to dance together and look alike. I was doing some soloist

roles but not promotional ones," that is, parts that could lead to a promotion. "When I had my growth spurt—when I was 13, 14, and 15—I couldn't turn at all. I was totally wonky. I have attention deficit hyperactivity disorder, and one teacher told me I'd never be a dancer because of it. But now I'm on a medication that helps me to focus a lot.

"I could have been a basketball player, but who wants to be around a bunch of men all day? Now I'm around a lot of gorgeous girls. People in school, especially on the football team, used to kid me about dancing. I said, 'You're sweating and feeling each other up, and I'm handling pretty girls all day.' In sports it's okay to make things look hard. With ballet it's really physically hard, and you have to make it look easy."

He adds, "I wish there were more people in America who supported ballet. I was in a grocery store in Stuttgart when I was doing an apprenticeship with Stuttgart Ballet. I was wearing a Stuttgart Ballet T-shirt. This woman came up to me and was majorly impressed, just because I was a dancer. In the rest of the world people look up to you for being a ballet dancer." Of course, most people have to look up to Bo Busby anyway.

James Whiteside

James Whiteside is a second soloist from Milford, Connecticut. He says, "I met Mikko through the summer program here in 2001, when I was 17. I finished high school via correspondence classes while I was already a dancer. It was tough coming home at 6:30 and doing English homework when I just wanted to make dinner and go to bed.

"My parents were supportive. I had tried basketball and football when I was still at home, but it just wasn't working. At 9 years old I was doing jazz and tap. I started ballet lessons at 10 or 11. In 2002 Mikko hired me for BB II. At the end of the BB II year I was offered a job with the main company because they had an extra contract for a corps position. After I'd gotten a BB II contract here, I auditioned for Ballet West and got an offer for a corps position there. But I chose Boston because it was closer to home. When I was first in the corps here, there was no second soloist rank. Mikko created the second soloist position for older dancers who were in the corps but actually had outgrown corps roles."

He's getting good opportunities: major roles in *Giselle* and Elo's *Plan to B,* about as wide a range of ballet parts as you could think of. "In the last *Nutcracker* I was cast in eleven different parts. I was really stressed out." As for dancing *Plan to B,* he says, "It's so exhausting that sometimes I feel I'm going to vomit at the end." Despite the stresses, both psychological and physiological, he's rather relaxed about his career. "I take class five days a week or maybe six. Some people take class seven days a week. The school operates every day, and company members can take whatever classes they want." Does he do the cross-training that's so popular with ballet dancers now? "No, I don't really have the time. I'd like to go to the gym, but I have a very full plate." The main ingredient on that plate is getting cast in a great many parts because of his versatility. He says that sometimes he learns by watching tapes of other dancers in the roles he's going to play.

Unlike many ballet dancers who think they have arrived when taken into a major company, Whiteside is already thinking beyond ballet. "I'd love to go to school," he says, adding that he would like to study biology or chemistry. "I don't want to be dancing when I'm past my prime. I believe that I'll know when it's time to leave."

Heather Myers

Heather Myers, a second soloist from Calgary, Canada, did not have the problem of juggling ballet and academics that Whiteside experienced. Canada's National Ballet has an academic/ballet program. The Canadian government funds it. The teaching is patterned after the syllabus at London's Royal Ballet School, so along with classical ballet, Myers learned the polonaise, the mazurka, flamenco, and other national styles that have a big presence in the nineteenth-century classics that are a staple of the National Ballet's repertory. In Boston, Myers says that having learned flamenco "comes in handy with *Don Quixote,*" getting up and demonstrating the deeply arched back of a Spanish dancer.

"I spent three years studying at the National Ballet. I was 11 when I started. I never remember thinking of doing anything else. But after those three years, they turned me away because my proportions weren't right. So I spent a year at home. Then I went to the Royal Winnipeg Ballet's school for three years." She defends her height, which is 5'5", not much above average for an American woman, but tall for a classical ballet dancer, especially one in Boston Ballet, where Nissinen seems to favor short women and tall men. For instance, she says, "It's nice to have one or two tall, strong women to do Balanchine's *Rubies.*"

After Winnipeg, Myers auditioned in Europe for six months. But when it was announced that Nissinen was taking over in Alberta, she went back to Canada. "Before that I wouldn't have joined Alberta Ballet," she says. "I wanted something bigger." When Nissinen took on Boston, he invited her to come along, too.

Back in Calgary she had already begun choreographing small pieces for workshops. In Boston, Nissinen asked her for ideas. The only real restriction was that the ballet wouldn't require a full orchestra. By the terms of Boston Ballet's contract with the musicians' union, one program a year can be done without the full orchestra, which not only saves money but also gives opportunities to choreographers who want to use electronic music or a chamber quartet or just a piano. For her first time choreographing for a big company, she chose familiar music, even daring and dangerously familiar music, like the slow movement from Schubert's string quartet *Death and the Maiden.*

Unlike some choreographers, with Balanchine heading the list, she doesn't arrive at rehearsals for her works without any steps in mind. At Boston Ballet, the time it would take to choreograph in the studio, with dancers waiting around as the choreographer seeks inspiration, would be prohibitively costly. In the spring of 2007 she said, "I work things out beforehand, not in the studio." For her premiere for Boston, "I can't even start rehearsing until mid-January," she says, looking eager to get started.

Misa Kuranaga

"I was born in the Year of the Pig," says Misa Kuranaga. "It's embarrassing." The year was 1983, and the place was Osaka, Japan. Kuranaga's career has soared since she joined Boston Ballet in 2003. She was "discovered" by Nissinen at the 2002 Monaco Dance Forum, an event that she describes as "a dancer's market. We take class and show what we can do. I got other offers, from the Birmingham Royal Ballet and the Dutch National Ballet. But I was studying at the School of American Ballet [the feeder school for the New York City Ballet] at the time, and I wanted

Misa Kuranaga.
Photo by Wally
Gilbert.

to keep on doing Balanchine. The European companies have different systems. Once you start in a system you want to keep going in it."

Growing up in Japan in the 1980s, "I was the only one in the family who wanted to run around all the time," Kuranaga says. "My mom didn't know what to do with all my energy. My friends in kindergarten took ballet at a culture center. They loved it: the idea of the tiaras, the tutus, the toe shoes. They told us about toe shoes, and I kept imagining what they were for.

"I begged my mom to let me start ballet. I was 7 years old, and it was just a culture center," she says, describing something like an American YWCA. Nonetheless, it got her started in ballet. "The first year I was taking just two classes a week. My teacher asked my mother if I had taken any real ballet classes before. Then the teacher created a pre-professional class just for me. There were other students in it, but my teacher said she wouldn't create this class if I wouldn't be in it."

In 1993 she began attending the frequent ballet competitions in Japan, as a way to get noticed and perform before different audiences and judges. "We don't have a big famous ballet company yet in Japan, so we have all these competitions. If you win a gold medal, you have a better chance of getting into a foreign company." She entered many competitions in Japan. "Competition gives you confidence. You can get onstage in some very hard conditions sometimes. I went back to Japan last summer, and now the competitions are giving out a lot of scholarships so students can study in foreign countries." When Kuranaga was doing the Japanese competitions, none of them was giving away scholarships. The only way to get a scholarship was to enter the Prix de Lausanne in Switzerland. Unlike other competitions, this one is mainly for advanced students rather than professionals: the prize is a year spent in a prominent ballet troupe of the winner's choice. In 2001 Kuranaga won a scholarship at Lausanne. "Going to the Royal Ballet was my first choice, but someone else had already picked it." The prize lets only one winner go to a particular company in a particular year. "San Francisco Ballet was my second choice, so that's where I went, for a year's apprenticeship." She didn't make it into San Francisco Ballet. But by the end of her apprenticeship, although her early training had been a mixture of Japanese, Russian, and European techniques, she was wedded to the Balanchine style. So she headed east to study at its source, the School of American Ballet, which he had founded to train dancers for his New York City Ballet.

New York City Ballet, San Francisco Ballet, and Boston Ballet are all devoted to the Balanchine style. So is Kuranaga. On the face of it, it's a strange choice for her. Balanchine preferred tall women because they make a bigger physical impression onstage. Kuranaga is 5'2"("wardrobe thinks I'm 5'1¾"," she says ruefully) and the smallest dancer in Boston Ballet. So she isn't a natural candidate for the Balanchine technique, with its characteristic amplification of steps. While her appearance— dark hair pulled back, a pensive demeanor—qualifies her for the spritely Lise in *La Fille mal gardée* or the supernatural lead in *La Sylphide,* she also excels in such Balanchine ballets as *The Four Temperaments,* where she becomes authoritative, her body looking longer than it is. She's stubborn and opinionated, as her unlikely attachment to Balanchine shows. She also points out that being short has some advantages in ballet. Short dancers are likely to be better turners than tall ones. "Being compact helps us to get around easily," she says.

She's known in the company as a hard worker, someone who's in the studio at night and on weekends, practicing. Just before leaving for Boston Ballet's Spanish tour in the summer of 2007, she was in a studio helping some students. They stayed so late that the building was about to close, with Kuranaga and the students locked in for the night. She had to call for help on the cell phone she's glad she had with her.

Her parents traveled once to Boston to see her in *Nutcracker*. And she's traveled back to Japan to be a guest artist in a show in her hometown. "Now I think that there will be bigger and better ballet companies in Japan. I'd love to guest there more, but I don't want to go back permanently."

She's so mentally tough that she puts a positive spin even on an injury. "Last year I had a stress fracture on my left foot. I had to be out for six weeks. I missed *Don Quixote*. It was my first injury and my last," she says in a steely tone of voice. "But once it was over I was stronger physically and mentally."

The spring 2006 season saw her version of *A Star Is Born* when she stood in for Ponomarenko in *La Fille mal gardée,* which earned her critical raves. She went on to win the women's gold medal at the 2006 USA International Ballet Competition in Jackson, Mississippi. One of the most prestigious of the competitions around the world that often catapult young talent into ballet's big time, Jackson is held every four years, like the Olympics, and has blossomed to take its place alongside renowned competitions like those in Moscow, Tokyo, and Varna, Bulgaria. Nissinen and other directors are frequent judges at these events. It is a way for them, in addition to giving out medals, to play talent scout, finding new dancers for their companies.

Dancers in competitions generally have to choose from a prescribed list of classics along with contemporary pieces to perform. In the latter category Kuranaga danced short pieces by Jorma Elo and Viktor Plotnikov. One of her classical entries was the Black Swan pas de deux, in which she was partnered by Boston Ballet corps member Daniel Sarabia, who had a hand in the selection. The Black Swan, Odile, is all sultry malevolence. "At Boston Ballet the roles I always get to do are soft and cute," Kuranaga said in an interview in Boston Ballet's in-house publication, *Sightlines*. "I've never gotten to be sexy or evil. So I thought I would mess up as the Black Swan." She overcame her doubts, though, and "now I don't think those kinds of roles are my weakness at all. That's the biggest thing for me—more than the gold medal."

Misa Kuranaga and Reyneris Reyes rehearsing *Le Corsaire* for Mikko Nissinen. Photo by Wally Gilbert.

Sabi Varga

The most dramatic role that soloist Sabi Varga played in the spring 2006 season was himself. On April 30, while rehearsing the male pas de quatre from *Raymonda* for the company's forthcoming Russian program, Varga collapsed. It wasn't the usual sprain, strain, torn cartilage, or other injury common among dancers. No doctor could diagnose it. He suffered more from the spinal tap than from the actual collapse, about which he says, "The worst thing was that it felt like someone was pulling the eyes out of my head. I collapsed on the barre. I could only eat boiled eggs and this nutrition drink, until I was given a blood patch, which took effect right away. I was six days in bed." After the six days, though, he rose like Lazarus in order to return to the theater. His wife, soloist Melanie Atkins, was virtually carrying him, recalls Elo, who was rehearsing for the premiere of *Carmen*. Varga was soon back to normal. No one ever found out what the problem had been.

"Jorma had created the part of Escamillo on me," Varga says, "and I desperately wanted to do it." On May 12, 2006, he did. Elo was amazed. "He looked like he couldn't even stand up, but when he got onstage he did the part full-out, with no caution or stinting." Varga is one of Elo's favorites in Boston Ballet, partly because he works so hard. He's known for extreme virtuosity, but, Elo says, "he'll do some huge jump and instead of working the audience for applause after it, he just looks sort of surprised at what he's done."

Varga began studying dance in his hometown, Győr, in northwest Hungary, when he was 6. When he was 9 he begged his parents to let him go to the Hungarian Dance Academy in Budapest. "I actually went on a one-day hunger strike before they allowed me to go to the audition. I was scared. My mom said, 'If you don't like it, you don't have to stay.'" He liked it, and he stayed. "The government paid for everything," he says. "There are exams every six months, eighteen times until you can graduate. After nine years you'd dance a role in the Hungarian National Opera House." At that first audition, when he was 9, there were 3,000 boys and girls participating. Only 32 boys were accepted, and only 4 finished the entire program. "I'm the only one dancing in America," he says. "The others are still in Hungary. I was offered a job in the Hungarian National Ballet. The director wanted me for the company, but Mikko also made me an offer. My teacher said, 'Go with Mikko.'" So

Sabi Varga rehearsing *Raymonda*, act 3.
Photos by Wally Gilbert.

Varga went to Canada, while Nissinen was still head of Alberta Ballet. After Nissinen moved to Boston, he asked Varga to join him there. "At first I needed a lot of help to become a professional. I was really young, almost clownish. I wanted to stand out, to have a wonderful career. Mikko did a great job with me. He told me I was a diamond in the rough. I felt about him that he was a director in the rough. I feel that in the seven years I've been with Mikko I've learned a lot from him. And I think he's learned something from me.

"I was 21 when I came to Boston. In Alberta there weren't really ranks, so I wasn't a principal there. When I came to Boston Mikko put me in the corps, but I started by doing the leading role in Rudi van Dantzig's *Romeo and Juliet* with Sarah Lamb." Lamb is now a principal with England's Royal Ballet.

"I do like story ballets, and having a character," says Varga. "In Balanchine it's always about the girl—no mistake. It's not about the boys. I'm a very emotional person. When I was understudying Albrecht [the leading male role in *Giselle*], in the part where I'm on the floor, dying, and Giselle's picking up my hand and holding it to her heart, I started crying."

Varga's wife, Melanie, also performed in Calgary with Nissinen and then moved to Boston. (Several of the Boston dancers are married to fellow company members, which makes their weird schedules bearable. At least they're together.) While Varga is still in his mid-twenties, with at least a decade of first-rate performing to go, barring another mystery disease, he is already planning another career. "Sabi Varga, Photographer," says the sleek black business card he holds out. He's been promoted to first soloist, but he's casual about it and the prospect of one day becoming a principal. "It's just a couple more bucks and a title," he says. "You dance to see the reaction of the audience. And it's a live thing, a memory that stays with you, and with the audience, too, you hope. It's never the same twice."

One sad or even demeaning reality of the lives of ballet dancers who have trained for a decade or more just to be in the corps is that with a contract of forty-one weeks a year, as Boston Ballet's was in 2006–07, they have to find other work during the layoffs and breaks or else apply for unemployment insurance. "At least," quips Varga, "you can file for unemployment online now."

Lorna Feijóo and Nelson Madrigal

Feijóo and Madrigal, both born in the mid-1970s and trained in Havana, Cuba, are an illustration of careers dictated, and then liberated, by communist politics, like those of Ponomarenko and Plotnikov.

Cuban ballet bonded with Russian communism in 1959, with Fidel Castro's revolution. Like the Soviet government, the new regime in Cuba decided that ballet could be used as a symbol of progress rather than an emblem of times past. The Cuban ballerina Alicia Alonso, one of the greatest dancers of the twentieth century, had traveled back and forth from her native Havana to New York and London, training and performing with illustrious companies. Alonso became an international superstar and also the director of the National Ballet of Cuba.

Feijóo and Madrigal grew up in the company's school, where Feijóo's mother was a teacher and where, by the time Feijóo started studying at age 10, Alonso was more active in the company than in the school. "There was a head of school who decided on the methodology for all of Cuba. The school program was five years, and then there was a test to see if you made it into the professional school that takes another three years. The professional school only takes fifteen students. In Cuba, ballet is a career, not a hobby." She leaves the "not like in the United States" part hanging in the air.

Alonso's influence did leave a mark on Feijóo, although the younger ballerina didn't study directly under the legendary one. "But I watched," Feijóo says. "She would coach *Swan Lake* and *Giselle,* and it would take two or three months to learn a role, not just a week." (There's another "not like here" implied.) "She would talk about the characters in a ballet, about how they felt. She said she had once danced forty-eight *Giselle*s in two months, and the way she kept being interested in it was 'I didn't dance them all the same.'"

She and Madrigal graduated into the National Ballet of Cuba. She finds that economically there is little difference between dancing in Havana and dancing in Boston, because although the economy in Cuba is poor, "school is free, medicine is free. And we got to tour a lot to festivals to earn money. We would do six months of the year touring. It's good not just because of the money but because you need to see other dancers and other choreography."

It was the "other choreography" that made Feijóo and Madrigal leave Cuba for good, she says. She had wanted to dance works she had seen in other countries, including Sir Kenneth MacMillan's *Manon* and the Balanchine repertory. "I really wanted to do contemporary ballets, too," she says. She has had plenty of them to do in Boston. Nonetheless, "I really miss Cuba. Latin people are really close to their families. I call my mother every day, and sometimes we have conference calls with the rest of the family. We waited for four years to get green cards." This document is crucial to foreign dancers in American companies because it allows them to travel back and forth between their native countries and here.

Feijóo is something of a diva, with a personal agent in California to promote her. Boston Ballet anticipated a bonanza of free national publicity when the *Today* show devoted a lengthy segment of a spring 2006 program to Lorna and her sister, Lorena, a principal dancer with San Francisco Ballet. They had danced together only once before, when Nissinen cast them both in *Swan Lake,* in the dual Odette/Odile role usually played by a single ballerina.

From the standpoint of Boston Ballet, the *Today* show was a colossal bust. The words *Boston Ballet* were never mentioned, nor was the name of choreographer Val Caniparoli, although what the sisters were dancing was an excerpt of his popular *Lambarena*, an amalgam of African dance and music and classical ballet set to Bach. To anyone unfamiliar with ballet, *Today*'s producers included, it might appear that the sisters were inventing this extremely popular choreography as they went along and just happened to be in perfect unison. The lack of credits suggested that a ballerina of Lorna Feijóo's stature didn't hold a position connected with a major company and that no one had choreographed *Lambarena*.

The *Today* show incident is an illustration of how difficult it is to popularize classical ballet in America. The Feijóo sisters' latest foray into that territory is their appearance on *Sesame Street* scheduled for its fall 2008 season.

7

The Artistic Associate

In 2002, when she visited Boston to see Stanton Welch's production of *Madame Butterfly,* Trinidad Vives was associate director at Houston Ballet, which was going to do *Butterfly* the next season. She and Nissinen had dinner, and in short order Nissinen offered her a job. One motivation to move east was that the director in Houston, Ben Stevenson, was retiring, and there was uncertainty about who would replace him. (It turned out to be Welch.)

"I'd been in Houston for eight years," she says, "and I thought maybe it was time for a new start. It was shocking to me that Mikko offered me a job so quickly, because he didn't know me." Vives is from Madrid, and "Boston seemed like a more European city than Houston, with more culture."

She had been to Boston before, to stage Stevenson's *Dracula,* one of the brand-name ballets that boards of trustees think will succeed at the box office. Staging *Dracula* for several companies launched Vives into the world of the répétiteur.

The biggest difference between Houston Ballet and the Boston company, she says, is that "in Houston the director was and is a choreographer. First Ben, now Stanton. After Ben, the board wanted another choreographer." A choreographer/director "feels that the company is a vehicle for his work," Vives says. Stevenson is British, with a predilection for full-length story ballets. Besides *Dracula* and *Cleopatra,* attempts to exploit popular themes notoriously lacking in real choreography, he had choreographed a *Cinderella, Sleeping Beauty, Swan Lake,* and others. He invited fellow Britons to choreograph and Margot Fonteyn to advise the company. "Because Ben is British," Vives says, "the company was more old-fashioned and expressive. The technical side was emphasized less."

Vives met Stevenson when she was dancing in his *Cinderella* at English National Ballet. She was going to dance in Houston, too, but she became pregnant, and Stevenson offered her a ballet mistress job instead. While admiring Boston's similarity to a European city, she cites Houston's economic advantages. "When Ben came," she says, "it was boom time in Texas. The board built this huge endowment that carries them through the bad times." In the 1980s, one of the "bad" times economically, Houston built the Wortham Theater Center, funded to the tune of $66 million by the private sector. The facility features two theaters, one with 2,423 seats, the other with 1,100 seats. It seems an ideal set-up: there's even underground parking. The Wortham is home to the Houston Ballet and the Houston Grand Opera. When visiting companies, including American Ballet Theatre, come to Houston, they perform at another facility.

Vives has experienced many different styles and syllabi and says she tries to take the best of each, which is the general philosophy behind Nissinen's Boston Ballet. *Purity* and *squareness* are words she uses to describe Boston's training. She contrasts it with what's taught at the School of American Ballet. "It gets extreme at SAB," she says, sitting in her Boston Ballet office and demonstrating what she means by "extreme." She flings her arm backwards and arches her wrist. Then she does "squareness," letting her arm assume a more neutral position, falling gently from her shoulder, not calling attention to itself.

"If you don't have that squareness," she says, "you have a harder time doing the extreme steps when you need to." And there are a lot of extreme steps in the Boston repertory, by choreographers from Balanchine to Jorma Elo, Mark Morris, Helen Pickett, Twyla Tharp, and others. The idea behind the teaching of Nissinen and his associates is to prepare dancers to perform a variety of styles, adapting to each.

Vives champions the idea that each dancer should be an individual. "Ben used to say, 'Don't try to be Margot Fonteyn. Be yourself,'" she recalls. "When Maina Gielgud was in Boston doing *Giselle,* she made sure the corps wasn't just a machine. There are eighteen girls dancing the same steps, but they're all different artists, too, and each has a particular presence."

The ultimate vehicle for self-expression in Boston Ballet's 2006–07 season was *The Dying Swan,* the famous solo that Mikhail Fokine created for Anna Pavlova in 1907. Vives coached three Boston Ballet principals in the role: Karine Seneca, Lorna Feijóo, and Romi Beppu. "They come from entirely different backgrounds," Vives says. "Karine was the most reserved. She's having this intimate moment with herself that pulls the audience in. Lorna is more expressive. She has no fear about doing things her own way. Romi is the youngest and least experienced. She was more hesitant. She thought, 'Is it going to be wrong?' She needed to feel safe. She matured with the experience. The three dancers responded differently to the music" [which is from Camille Saint-Saëns's *Carnival of the Animals*]. It depended on when they wanted to take a deep breath or make a big arm gesture. I didn't really correct," Vives says. "I just made suggestions."

Beppu watched tapes of some of her great predecessors in the role, including Maya Plisetskaya, Natalia Makarova, and Gelsey Kirkland, to see what she did and didn't like. "Some of it gets melodramatic," she says. "It's scary because it's so simple and so emotional." In rehearsal Vives urged Beppu to suffer more, so that she came to a poignant near-collapse and then found momentary strength to revive briefly before her demise. It didn't work. "I'm sure it will be much easier to do onstage," Vives said reassuringly, recognizing how hard it is to summon extreme emotion in a well-lit rehearsal room as opposed to a darkened stage.

Vives doesn't mind her transition from dancer to ballet mistress in the least. She teaches company class two or three times a week. "Then I rehearse from 11:30 to 6:30. In the lunch hour I discuss things like casting with Mikko. He respects my opinion. It's a conversation, not a dictatorship." In one tense lunch hour, Vives burst into Nissinen's office with the bad news that two of the three men dancing the part of Don José in Elo's new *Carmen* were now out of commission with injuries. Nissinen was preternaturally calm. "If I panic," he said, "imagine the trickle-down effect."

While Vives's role isn't something the general public is aware of, an even less known but critical role is that of the artistic coordinator/ballet master, better known as the scheduler. Boston Ballet's scheduler is Shannon Parsley. "I'm the hub of information for everyone," she explains with a modest giggle. Parsley is herself a dancer, formerly with Miami City Ballet and still performing with the Suzanne Farrell Ballet, so she has experienced her current job from the other side.

Parsley sorts out the various requests of choreographers, ballet masters, the wardrobe department, public relations, marketing, and other departments and individuals: all need studio space and dancers' time for their activities. The company may work on as many as eight ballets in a single day, and most of the dancers are in more than one piece. Choreographers and répétiteurs working with large casts need bigger studios than those working on a pas de deux. The daily company class at 9:45 a.m. always gets the largest studio. Sometimes the studios are rented out for functions—an organization's lunch or filming a movie. "The studios are always busy. We had Mick Jagger come in and rent a studio to work on the dancing part of his tour. *Extreme Home Makeover* also did a piece here. I have to make out a schedule that fits all this in. I have to make sure a dancer isn't scheduled for more than one rehearsal at a time." The schedule, which is a grid with the seven studios listed on the top line and what's going on in them at what time in the blocks underneath, is posted two days in advance, in accordance with the regulations of the dancers' union, the American Guild of Musical Artists, which also stipulates that dancers have to have a five-minute break in each hour and that they can't rehearse for more than three consecutive hours.

There wouldn't be any point in making out the schedule any earlier than two days ahead of time anyway, because things are always in a state of flux. "If a dancer calls in sick, I have to do it all over again," Parsley says. Ditto for when the casting for a ballet changes. A coach may need more time or time with different dancers. (They never seem to need less.) Parsley also has to work appointments for costume fittings into the equation. She has to take into account the availability of the choreographer, the répétiteur, pianists, and the Boston Ballet artistic staff member who will be in charge of ongoing rehearsals after the choreographer or répétiteur has left. She has to be a cross between a computer and a chess master.

"I work directly with Trini," Parsley says. "My office and Trini's are right next to each other, and we're yelling back and forth all the time. By the end of the day, it becomes apparent what needs to be done the next day, depending on how successful the rehearsals have been. Usually, ballet masters and choreographers will go to Trini's office and ask for what they need.

"I could probably do this job without e-mail, but it would be a lot more work. I'd say it's half and half, e-mails and running around the building. Sometimes it gets a little crazy."

8

The Director of the School

The purpose of Boston Ballet's affiliated school has always been an issue. With three branches, it is the largest ballet school in North America. That's not necessarily good for the quality of the company. "At the moment," says Tamara King, the principal of the branch of the school in suburban Newton, "our school is a revenue-generating program. That's why it's so big and why it doesn't produce many professional dancers. Anyone can take classes."

There *are* a few young people who have come through the school and gone into BB II, she notes. BB II consists of eight to ten young people, all hoping to join the main company or another troupe on that level. The BB II dancers are also useful in all-hands-on-deck situations such as *The Nutcracker* or *Swan Lake,* which call for large corps de ballet.

"The biggest goal of the school now is to start increasing the number of dancers who become professionals," says King. "But this is still an organization with a lot of pressure to produce money to help support the company."

In the spring of 2007, Nissinen took a major step toward increasing the quality of the school by hiring Margaret Tracey, a former principal dancer with New York City Ballet, to run and revamp it. Tracey was trained at NYCB's affiliate School of American Ballet by legendary teachers, including Alexandra Danilova and Antonia Tumkovsky. "Tumi built your strength," says Tracey. Dancers of all ages and levels braved her famously difficult classes as preparation for taking on the most challenging Balanchine roles. Tumkovsky had plenty of stamina as well. She died in 2007, at age 101, having retired at age 98. There is

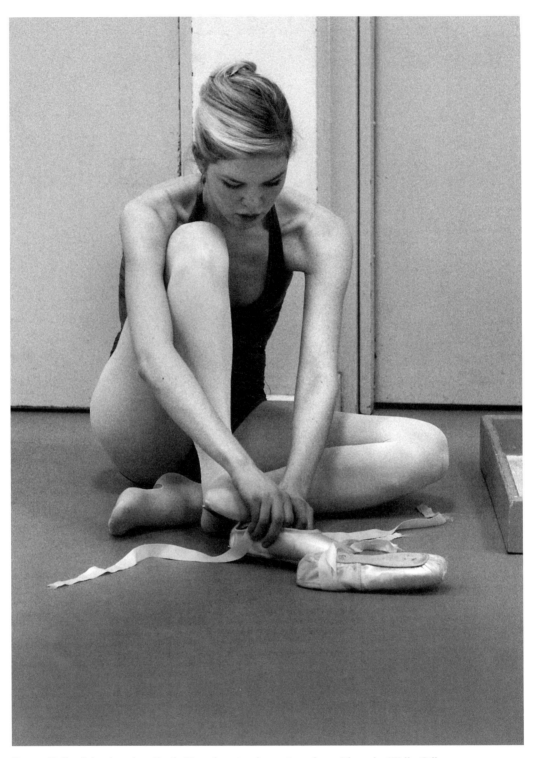

Boston Ballet School student Emily Tyra changing her pointe shoes. Photo by Wally Gilbert.

a DVD of her teaching that will preserve at least part of her method. Danilova, among the earliest of Balanchine's muses, died in 1997 at age 93. "Danilova taught you about your artistry and the glamour of being a ballerina," Tracey says.

"The aesthetic I learned from them and from others at SAB is the basis of what I'll be doing in Boston," she says, while sitting in her office with a syllabus she's working on for the company. "Mikko asked me to do a syllabus for other teachers to follow. I want to train a ballet dancer who can go anywhere and perform anything." The consistency of training that Tracey's syllabus will lead to if it is successful will mean that for the first time students in the school will comprehend a step in the same way. The ultimate hope is to produce dancers who don't have to be retrained as they come up the ranks in Boston. As with SAB's written syllabus, which also exists in video form, Tracey's will be for the exclusive use of the Boston school. There are plenty of widely available tapes and DVDs of famous dancers and ballet teachers demonstrating their versions of classical ballet. There are mixed opinions, though, about their usefulness. They don't make accommodation for individual bodies, for instance, as a good teacher does in a live class setting. At best, they're an adjunct. At worst, following them could even result in injury.

Just as Tracey arrived at Boston Ballet, the school was for the first time able to offer a dormitory to students who don't live in the Boston area, along with academic classes that wouldn't conflict with their ballet training. During her years as a student at SAB, Tracey lived on her own in New York. Natalie Glebov, another SAB legend, "convinced my father that I'd be fine," Tracey says with a smile. Tamara King holds a more conventional view. "It's a disaster having 16- and 17-year-olds living on their own in a city," she says. Hence the Grace Performing Arts Academy, located within easy walking distance of the ballet's studios. The academy was the brainchild of Susan St. John, an experienced teacher who had already been the resident director of Boston Ballet's Summer Dance Program for five years and knew what she was getting into. Boston Ballet, with its ongoing financial problems, couldn't fund the venture, so St. John started it as her own business. The academy is open not only to ballet students but also to students studying other arts in the Boston area and to preprofessional athletes as well.

9

The General Manager

Boston Ballet's dancers were on layoff for most of the month of June 2007, collecting unemployment insurance, teaching, or performing guest stints with other companies. In the same month, ballet general manager David Tompkins said that he wouldn't get a day off until January, when *Nutcracker* was over. He and others from the administrative side of the company were working at the time with a firm of consultants. "They were looking at every aspect of the business," Tompkins said, "the school, the dancers, the administration."

Tompkins speaks from the down-to-earth perspective of a midwesterner. He's from Kansas City. Almost thirty years ago he entered the so-called glamorous world of the performing arts, in fields ranging from rock music to musical comedy to ballet. He's worked with Ballet West in Utah, Orlando Ballet in Florida, and, since 2004, Boston Ballet. He believes that the American public doesn't understand ballet as easily as it does symphonic music. "Kids grow up playing a musical instrument. But ballet is still perceived as something for an upper socioeconomic group. There's still a stigma attached to it. People think it's effete, not athletic." He recounts the occasion when, while working at Ballet West, he put together a group of male dancers and a baseball farm team called the Trappers, and the ballplayers found that they could not survive a ballet class. "The experiment was televised for several nights. It was really a public relations ploy," Tompkins says. It was hardly the only attempt, both recent and not so recent, to convince Americans that ballet is a macho endeavor. Among recent examples was the 2003 PBS documentary *Born to Be Wild: The Leading Men of American Ballet Theatre*. When the teenage boys in Boston Ballet's 2007 summer course were force-marched into a ballet history lecture that ended with the ABT program, most of them skipped lunch to finish watching the show. Their vocal and physical enthusiasm suggested they were watching an athletic event.

Tompkins speaks about another aspect of a changing mentality about the arts. "When I was in school, I'd do anything to be onstage. I paid for my own parking, and I bought my own makeup. It was a whole different way of participating in the arts. In the mid-1990s, when I was at Ballet West, I wanted to use local students as extras—parts like the king and queen—and they were thrilled. 'Yes!' 'Anything you want!' Later they started asking me how much it paid. 'My time isn't free,' they'd say. I've spent a lot of time with small and medium-sized companies. The coming of the unions has been the biggest change. When I was in Orlando, they were transitioning into a professional company with unions. Before that, the show wouldn't have gone on if they didn't have volunteers—and me sewing costumes."

At Boston Ballet, Tompkins deals with the production staff both in-house and from the theater. The company manager, Kristin Hwang, is his liaison with the dancers. Along with the director of the school, she is also responsible for the child supervisor and six assistants who cope with the 250 children who appear in the multiple casts of *The Nutcracker*. Tompkins is a problem solver, especially when the company transfers into the theater. Overtime is one of the toughest issues, and he says that the dancers union, not the musicians or stagehands union, is the hardest to deal with. While Shannon Parsley's schedules show what the dancers will be doing in two days' time, Tompkins's focus is on the moment at hand.

"I have to find a solution to things like a choreographer who wants overtime for the dancers," he says. "I have to make sure that choreographers give the dancers their five-minute breaks. Sometimes, to save on overtime, the orchestra goes home and the dancers will rehearse with a piano. And I can say to the dancers, 'Everyone who is not in the last scene can go home now,' so my overtime will be less. It doesn't occur frequently, but it can happen." He sees one upside of cutting down on overtime. "People used to do three- and four-act ballets with long intermissions. Now, partly because of the threat of paying overtime, they've shortened the ballets and cut out much of the mime that nobody understood anyway."

Like many people who work with ballet companies in capacities other than dancing, Tompkins has picked up aspects of the art simply by years of watching. "Did you know," he asks, "that guys with long arms have much more difficulty with lifts than guys with short arms? It's that much further to the arm-lock position for the guys with long arms."

10

The Répétiteurs

You want to take the pulse of the ballet world? Ask a répétiteur, also called a stager, the person who has the responsibility of teaching a work to a company and making it come out as close as possible to the choreographer's wishes. Répétiteurs are the delegates of the choreographers or their estates. Copyrights on ballets, as with other works of art, are in effect for seventy years after the choreographer's death. After that, people can adapt the original, or what remains of it. In the case of nineteenth-century ballets, they can do as they please. Hence the liberties taken with *Swan Lake,* some of them the equivalent of Shakespeare in modern dress. *Swan Lake* has been done with a male Swan Queen, in Matthew Bourne's award-winning 1995 production, and there are versions presenting the villainous Von Rothbart as a woman and Prince Siegfried as having an Oedipal relationship with his mother. About as radical as Boston Ballet has gotten with *Swan Lake* during Nissinen's reign was that one-off production in 2004 when he divided the dual role of the virtuous Odette and the evil Odile between the Feijóo sisters. "*Swan Lake* is the greatest classical ballet production in existence," he says. "Much of the original is still in place, and I didn't want to touch those parts, just the ones that time hadn't treated so kindly. I didn't set out to change *Swan Lake,* but rather to curate it."

On the other hand, some stagers feel a responsibility to try to preserve the original choreography of nineteenth-century ballets. The version of *Giselle* that Maina Gielgud taught to Boston Ballet doesn't stray far from what we've come to think of as the "original." And in Copenhagen, the Royal Danish Ballet is proud to have handed down its treasure trove of mid-nineteenth-century ballets by August Bournonville from one dancer to another in an unbroken, easily documented line. So the version of Bournonville's *La Sylphide* that Finnish-born Sorella Englund, the first foreigner to dance with the Royal Danish Ballet, taught to Boston Ballet is probably as authentic as it is possible to be, although in the program she cautiously describes her staging as "after Bournonville."

In order to produce ballets legally and/or authentically, ballet companies need stagers more than the stagers need them. The stagers are, after all, the repositories of invaluable knowledge. In some instances, such as Merrill Ashley and *Ballo della Regina,* a work Balanchine created for her and then bequeathed to her, they hold the copyright to the work. This gives them the freedom to speak their minds.

Ashley and Francia Russell, both former New York City Ballet dancers, worked with Boston Ballet on its "Classic Balanchine" program in the spring of 2007. Despite her ties with NYCB, Russell, who later went on to direct the Pacific Northwest Ballet in Seattle with her husband, Kent Stowell, is not one to genuflect to New York. She says rather forcefully that San Francisco, not NYCB or American Ballet Theatre, is currently the country's leading classical company.

Russell, retired from PNB, now travels the world staging Balanchine's works, chiefly those from the 1950s and 1960s, the period when she was dancing with NYCB. She was in Boston in 2007 to stage Balanchine's 1951 *La Valse.* Working directly with the master, Russell picked up the specific shadings of each gesture, and she believes she's able to give the choreography a period authenticity that later dancers who performed the same ballet cannot.

In the winter of 2007 she was glad to be in Boston. Her previous assignment was with the Bolshoi Ballet in Moscow, staging Balanchine's *Serenade* and teaching class every day. She's blunt about the experience. "There are so many dancers there who don't want to work. Some of them are bored civil servants. Every rehearsal I had to drag them off the floor. The performances were not great. One was a disaster. And it's Tchaikovsky, for heaven's sake. It's not Webern."

The director of the Bolshoi, Alexei Ratmansky, "is young and wonderful," Russell says. "But getting those dancers to change is like moving the *QE II.* And no one there even says hello, or do you know where your hotel is, or would you like a cup of coffee?" Boston Ballet is a different story, she says, a welcoming company.

She contrasts PNB with Boston Ballet. "There are a lot of really good male dancers in Boston, more than in Seattle. And there is a more traditional ballet style in Boston, with the men doing all those tricks. At PNB so many of the dancers were trained in our own school. In Boston it's less homogeneous, but there is great vigor." One thing the two companies have in common, she notes, is that both PNB and Boston are often not considered in the same league with bigger and better known companies on the same coasts. "People in Seattle used to go to San Francisco to see ballet," she says. "It took years to convince them that there was good ballet right at home." Boston has always faced the same problem with New York. There are balletomanes in Boston who would get on the shuttle flights to New York and see companies there rather than checking out what was at home. "In the past," Russell says, "that may have made sense. But now Mikko is in the process of forging a real company identity. This is one of the best companies in the country now. And it was not before."

Russell's route to becoming a Balanchine répétiteur was hardly straightforward. She's down-to-earth about her training, a page out of dance history. In Paris as a child she studied briefly with a legend in dance history, Mathilde Kschessinska, who had risen to the rank of prima ballerina assoluta at the Maryinsky in St. Petersburg in the 1890s. Kschessinska was a local girl made good. Very good. She had had affairs with Nikolai II, before he became Russia's last czar, and then with the Grand Duke Andrei, whom she married in Paris in 1921. "The Grand Duke would call our hotel and arrange my private ballet lessons in Kschessinska's apartment," Russell recalls, adding that although she appreciated this brush with history she didn't learn much.

Russell's peripatetic family moved to London so that Russell could attend the Royal Ballet School, which rejected the 12-year-old on grounds that she would grow to be too tall for ballet, a conclusion the school authorities came to after meeting her father, who measured 6'2". Besides, they told the disappointed child, her toes were too long. Balanchine, of course, liked tall dancers, and so, after a few more training adventures, Russell ended up at Balanchine's School of American Ballet in 1956—for three weeks. After that, Balanchine invited her to perform with NYCB, where she danced until 1964.

She also danced in several European companies but quit after a bad knee injury. "Surgery wasn't an option then for a woman on pointe. And besides, I wanted to go to college. My father had pushed me into dance," which is the opposite of the usual scenario involving parents steering their children to college rather than to a career in the arts. To college she went, then she worked at an art gallery and for a publisher. She explains why she quit performing: "I was never going to be the dancer I wanted to be. You have to be so focused on yourself, on your feet, your mind, your injuries, only on yourself." She, meanwhile, is happier talking about Rubens's drawings and staging Balanchine.

Equally devoted to Balanchine is Merrill Ashley, one of the most glorious ballerinas to have worked with the master in his later years. At one point Nissinen asked her about becoming a ballet mistress in Boston. "I wouldn't be good at it," she says. "I couldn't do the corps. My eye is more attuned to working with the soloists than with the corps. And there's the money problem in Boston. Mikko then asked me to come and be a Balanchine consultant. I was to instill the technique and ideology of Balanchine ballets, but that proved to be impossible financially as well.

"I think the company has continued to improve since Mikko took over," Ashley says. "He's raised the level amazingly. About the big turnover, you never know if it's because he didn't like some of the dancers he inherited or because they quit. But it's clearly a company he's formed now."

When Ashley came to Boston to stage *Ballo della Regina,* "There was a bit of a problem," she says. "I didn't know what the casting was. It was unfortunate the way things developed." Ashley says that she and Lorna Feijóo have a "special relationship" from the time Ashley worked in Cuba. Nissinen wanted to put a Boston principal in the male lead of *Ballo.* "I'd seen him do it, and I didn't think he was great. I ended up with some young boys after it became obvious to me that they were so much better in *Ballo* than the principals. For a while I didn't know who was dancing it. The rehearsal schedule was how everyone found out. It got ugly. I told Mikko what I felt. I didn't want to get caught in the middle of it." Another complication: "Lorna wanted to do it with Nelson [Madrigal, her husband, who was not the principal Nissinen originally nominated]. She was insulted that she didn't get to do it with him. I didn't want to apply pressure to get him the role," Ashley says. In the end, Feijóo's partner in *Ballo* was the young soloist James Whiteside.

"The communications between staff and dancers is a problem in every company I've ever worked with," Ashley says. She acknowledges that

Nissinen is good at talking with individual dancers and that "dancers have to be so self-centered, and just do what they do, that it's hard to take themselves out of the big picture."

There tend to be last-minute changes in casting in Boston Ballet, she says, "and the dancers don't have it explained to them. They haven't been respected in that."

As a true Balanchine disciple, Ashley has made videotapes on Balanchine technique, and her 1984 autobiography, *Dancing for Balanchine,* includes serial photographs of every split-second of particular steps done as she learned them from him. (They look like Eadweard Muybridge's famous stop-action photos proving that a galloping horse did indeed have all four legs off the ground at once.)

"I believe that the technique that Balanchine advocated is essential to his ballets. I see that whenever I stage *Ballo.* Inevitably, there are steps that don't suit a particular dancer. There are some steps that should never be touched, but sometimes modifying things slightly isn't the end of the world.

"I think a lot of dancers haven't been exposed to true Balanchine teaching," says Ashley, who can go into minute detail on the most basic steps as the master explained them. "A lot of it is misinterpreted Balanchine teaching. Then when they're doing the ballets, they can't do the steps, literally, especially at the tempo he demanded. If you can show them in a regular class, they start to understand it better. The kind of fitness and versatility that Balanchine technique creates in a dancer helps in performing Elo and Tharp. You become more aware of how you do everything, whether you're putting your foot down softly or harshly, depending on what's called for."

These days, Ashley teaches and coaches at NYCB. She has staged *Ballo* for just seven companies. "It's very hard to do, even for the soloists," she says. Her secret? "I could move fast because I have small feet."

11

The Medical Team

Lyle Micheli

All eight of the surgeries that former ballet principal dancer Viktor Plotnikov endured to keep on dancing in Boston Ballet were performed by Dr. Lyle Micheli, founder of the Sports Medicine Clinic at Children's Hospital in Boston, which is a second home to some of the dancers. "Viktor probably holds the record," Micheli says.

Either Micheli or one of his staff is at every Boston Ballet performance, a bonus to the dancers that not every ballet company can offer. On more than one occasion, Micheli has bounded out of his seat in the audience to rush backstage after a dancer has suffered an onstage fall or other injury. He was in the audience one night in the 1980s when Boston Ballet ballerina Marie-Christine Mouis was dancing in the Wang Theatre with Rudolf Nureyev. Nureyev dislocated her shoulder. Micheli jumped out of his seat in the audience, dashed backstage, and tended to her so she could go back onstage.

That was in the early days of the Dance Clinic at Children's, an outgrowth of the Sports Medicine Clinic that blossomed there beginning in the 1970s. Micheli, a former rugby player, was all too aware of athletic injuries, and he knew that dancers are, among other things, athletes.

The dancers at Boston Ballet face the same risks as those in other companies, but they have better health care than most except those with far greater resources, largely thanks to Micheli, who has been a ballet trustee for a quarter century and whose relationship with the ballet has served as a model for other companies around the country.

The dancers started coming to him at Children's in the mid-1970s. Not long afterward, some therapists trekked to the old parking garage in the South End where the company was then headquartered. "The dancers liked our approach," says Micheli, "because we got them back in the studio and performing as soon as possible. We met with the Ballet and began talking about a satellite clinic, which opened in the Ballet's 1991 building, on the site of the old parking garage where the dancers took class and rehearsed. When we started, there was just one therapist. Now there's one there each working day, and when the company is performing at the Wang, there is a physician and a physical therapist backstage at every performance. The treatments now are much more sophisticated than in past decades. There was a time early on when dancers would try to minimize injuries, dance over them, but I think that for the most part we've gotten over that now."

Micheli cites injuries that dancers are particularly prone to, which a less specialized physician might overlook. "One is a little extra bone at the back of the ankle," he says. "It can grow and become so severe that dancers lose their ability to point their feet. It's a flexor of the big toe. The tendon thickens until they can't move."

Micheli is high on cross-training now. "I think that supplementing traditional dance exercises by doing strength training with weights and machines is good," he says. He's also a fan of Pilates and Gyrotonics, which several former Boston Ballet dancers now teach.

"We assess each dancer at the beginning of the year," he says. "That program was temporarily cut because of budgetary concerns, but now we're back with it. We give each dancer an exercise prescription, which has proven very helpful."

"Men," Micheli observes, "get injured more than women. Girls generally start ballet earlier, and as a result, by the time they get to the professional level, you have a pretty refined instrument. We have a higher rate of injury in men because they tend to start later. So much for women as the weaker sex!"

Jared Redick is one Boston Ballet dancer who, despite Micheli's warnings, has danced while injured. He was the leading dancer in the Russian variation in Boston Ballet's *Nutcracker* in 2006. The faux Cossack choreography calls for kicks done from a squatting position and jumps with the legs doing the splits in the air. "One night," he says, "something popped in my knee. I knew something was really wrong, but I wanted to finish the show." Which he did. Backstage were the physician and physical therapist from Children's. They evaluated Redick's situation, iced his knee, and got him an appointment the next morning with Micheli.

"After *Nutcracker* we had a layoff and my knee felt fine," Redick says. "Then we started *A Midsummer Night's Dream.* I was Puck, which has lots of jumping. I had the best time doing that role. It's one of my all-time favorites. You jump, run around, and have fun. My knee hurt a lot, but I thought, I'll just try to make it through these shows." And he did. "Then I had surgery. The MRI I had had after *Nutcracker* showed a torn meniscus. Dr. Micheli only found out what was really wrong during the surgery. He found all this scar tissue right under my kneecap, which was why I couldn't straighten my knee all the way. He told me I would feel much better after the operation, and I did." (Plotnikov, on the other hand, says that some of the dancers feel that Micheli is a little too eager to operate.)

Redick is the very definition of "the show must go on." "I would rather dance until I absolutely can't anymore than go for surgery. A dancer's performing life is short." Still, he has had those three knee operations, the first when he was 19, in his first year as a corps dancer with San Francisco Ballet. "I tore my anterior cruciate ligament," he says. (Ballet dancers learn to speak medical jargon just as ballet physical therapists can explain the mechanics of a pirouette.) In less technical language Redick says that what happened in San Francisco was that "I blew out my knee in class. I was just beginning my career, and it took eighteen months to recover fully. It was more difficult emotionally than physically."

Ballet is a health hazard in the same sense that skiing and competitive skating are. Ballet dancers generally spend around ten years, from age 8 or 9, practicing things that later get their bodies into trouble. Repetitive movement, which wears down body parts, is the stuff of their daily lessons. They're taught to turn out their legs from their hip sockets until their feet are at a 180 degree angle, a totally unnatural position. The women learn to stand on their toes, which results in some of the world's ugliest and most deformed feet in people who are otherwise supremely beautiful. The men whirl through the air and in the worst case scenario land with a severed tendon and a severed career.

Micheli's attitude toward Ponomarenko's broken metatarsal was to wait it out. In the end, she missed not only the March 2006 performances but the entire spring season, which represents more than half of Boston's performance year. In the short career of a classical dancer, it's a hefty chunk of time to lose.

Mikko Nissinen's own career ended somewhat prematurely due to physical wear and tear. While still in San Francisco he developed two herniated disks and a hip problem. "I was 34," he says. "There was no point in continuing. I needed a hip replacement. I still haven't had one." The "Flying Finn," as he had been nicknamed by the Toronto press during a guest appearance there, was grounded.

Michelina Cassella

When Boston Ballet opened its new building in 1991, Micheli asked Michelina Cassella, one of the physical therapists on his staff at Children's, to move to Clarendon St. and start the satellite clinic there. Cassella was happy to say yes. "Fortunately," she says, "the opening also coincided with the renovation of the department at Children's. It used to be on two floors, but then it was consolidated onto one. So there was duplicate equipment, and the duplicates were transferred to the ballet. I felt very strongly that the equipment at the ballet should be Children's Hospital equipment, because it gets calibrated regularly by our bioengineering department. They check the whirlpools and the agitators, and make sure that the electrical contacts are safe. Whenever you have water and electricity together, you have to make sure it's safe. They also calibrate our ultrasound machine and our electrical stimulation equipment.

"Actually, we don't use the equipment all that much," Cassella says. "Mostly we use our hands." One of the dancer-specific methods she uses is iontophoresis, a means of delivering medication directly to the problem area without using a needle or taking it by mouth. "There's a little electrode pad where you put the medicine," she says. "Then you put the electrode on the injured spot. It's very effective with dancers, mostly for decreasing inflammation. Dancers get a lot of tendonitis because of overuse of particular body parts, all that repetitive motion."

When Cassella started the clinic at the ballet, she was frustrated by the insurance system. "The dancers have workers' compensation, but that's only for after an injury has occurred. I wanted to prevent injuries and also stop small injuries from becoming big ones." The solution was for the ballet to pay the full-time salary of a physical therapist from Children's. That way, insurance doesn't have to be an issue unless there is something so seriously wrong with a dancer that it requires hospitalization.

"Several articles have been written about how cost-effective our system is," Cassella says. Micheli notes that the financial benefits to the ballet are $100,000 a year. Instead of filling out seemingly endless forms for reimbursement, the dancers just write their names on a sign-up sheet, walk into the ballet's PT room, and get the treatment they need. "They really feel free to come into the therapy room because it doesn't involve any money on their part, and of course there is absolute confidentiality," Cassella says. In addition to a physical therapist being in the building every work day, Boston Ballet has a chiropractor, a nutritionist, an acupuncturist, and a psychologist on call. "We have dancers with psychological problems, and they feel free to come to us because of the confidentiality," Cassella says. "Also, a physician from Children's comes every Tuesday to the studio. They follow up injuries. They can write a prescription right away if needed, and they're available to the dancers at the hospital, too. They get to know them. They love doing the ballet. This is an exciting clinic."

She notes that "because one of us is always in the building, we're the triage. We're the first to look over the situation. If I see a dancer get injured, I can put them into a cab and they're at the hospital in twenty minutes, and Dr. Micheli or one of his colleagues sees them right away. Immediate injury care is crucial in recovery." When the Ballet is at the Wang, Cassella transfers her operation there, moving all her equipment so that she can be ready in the event of an emergency. "There have been things that have happened in dress rehearsals," she says, "and an immediate decision had to be made, not only for the dancer's treatment but because it's also a casting issue." The injured dancer has to be replaced by another dancer who may already have been dancing a different role, so that dancer has to be replaced as well, and it all has to be decided on the spot. If the injured dancer had been scheduled to do a pas de deux in the performance, the replacement dancer may not have rehearsed with the injured dancer's partner, adding another layer of complication. "Partnering has to be so precise," Cassella says, mentioning the lift called a "fish dive," in which the ballerina looks as if she's about to dive into the floor. If the timing isn't perfect, she just might do that.

Around the corner from the physical therapy room at Boston Ballet is the exercise room, with weights as well as Pilates, Gyrotonic®, and Body-Code exercise equipment. Aside from the latter strange-looking devices, it looks like a mini-version of the gyms where ordinary people work out before or after their sedentary 9 to 5 days. It used to be that the rigors of ballet itself were enough exercise for dancers. Then cross-training became popular for hitting the parts of the body that ballet alone does not. Old photographs of many male dancers show undeveloped chests and arms. Working out with weights has changed that. And it's not unusual to see dancers at Boston Ballet working out with big exercise balls during rehearsal breaks.

As far as other health problems go, the ballet profession is notorious for junk-food consumption and eating disorders. A decade or two ago, some ballet companies were known for insisting that their dancers be extra thin. Anorexia was a well-publicized problem at Boston Ballet after Heidi Guenther's death, even though it turned out that she died of an irregular heartbeat. Today there is less anorexia, Cassella says. "There's more awareness that this is a serious problem. But there's a big difference between disordered eating—some kinds of diets, for instance—and an eating disorder. We try to talk about eating healthy and not focusing on diets. There are lots of people who are naturally thin and don't have an eating disorder. How thin dancers are also depends on the aesthetic of the individual company. In modern dance companies, you can have more full-figured dancers.

"I'm actually more worried now about smoking than eating." One dancer in Boston Ballet estimates that 15–20 dancers in the company smoke. "I do wish we could get them to stop," Cassella says. "For one thing, it's much harder and it takes longer to heal stress fractures if you're a smoker. It's too bad that there are so many of them in Boston Ballet. If there are only one or two in a company, they feel embarrassed about it."

Cassella watches classes and rehearsals whenever possible and has become something of an expert in choreography herself. She analyzes the steps to determine whether it's the choreography itself or the repetitions of certain steps that have led to an injury. "Sometimes I'll say to a dancer, 'Can you just mark the steps in the rehearsal today?'" (Marking means not performing the choreography full out, to minimize stress on the injured body part.) She and her team also may make suggestions about casting decisions. If, during *Nutcracker,* a woman with a slight injury is in both the big set pieces for the corps, the "Snow" scene and the "Waltz of the Flowers," Cassella might ask if she could just do "Snow" and someone else could fill in for "Flowers." Redick says, "Someone else filling in is not easy in Boston Ballet. This is not that big a company. It's not like we have ninety dancers and there are extra people waiting in the wings." Redick and other dancers also feel that the extreme mix of styles that Boston Ballet dances contributes to injuries. Rehearsing half a dozen ballets a day, choreography from the nineteenth, twentieth, and twenty-first centuries, inevitably puts physical strain on the body.

"Sports medicine is still way ahead of us," Cassella laments. "In the sports pages in newspapers you're always getting detailed analyses of athletes' injuries, but you never get that with dancers. People just think that ballet is beautiful and easy because the ballerina is smiling. But she might be smiling on an injury. Football players don't have to smile. And look at all that padding they wear! A ballerina has just a few ounces of tights and tutu, which offer no protection at all."

Ballerinas may look fragile, but that's deceptive. Cassella singles out Larissa Ponomarenko, who weighs in at under 100 pounds. "But," Cassella notes, "she's really strong, really prepared for everything. Her partners love dancing with her because she practically lifts herself. I'd like to put Larissa up against a football player."

12

The Musicians

Boston is a music town, with the list of its dozens of musical institutions led by the world-renowned Boston Symphony Orchestra, the recipient of several eight-figure gifts. The $3.5 million bequest that former Boston Ballet trustee Dr. Beatrice Barrett left to the company at her death in 2003, the largest single gift in the troupe's history, was earmarked for two areas: the production of works by Balanchine and the endowment of the music director's position.

Jonathan McPhee

Jonathan McPhee has been the music director and principal conductor for Boston Ballet since 1988. From the beginning, the company made a commitment to dance to live music. "There were times, long ago, when the programs were better played than they were danced," says Richard Dyer, the former classical music critic at the *Boston Globe,* who has watched the ballet since the days of E. Virginia Williams. "The Boston Ballet orchestra has had a succession of very good conductors. Jonathan has upheld that tradition and added to it." McPhee's résumé is impressive indeed: he's conducted for Martha Graham, the Joffrey Ballet, New York City Ballet, the Royal Danish Ballet, England's Royal Ballet, the Australian Ballet, and other A list troupes around the world.

"A conductor doesn't go into the field thinking, 'Oh, I'm going to conduct ballet,'" McPhee says. "It's not an easy job. In some people's minds it is secondary to conducting a symphony or opera, and even within a ballet troupe the company doesn't think that it is the most nec-

Jonathan McPhee, music director of Boston Ballet. Photo by Wally Gilbert.

essary thing. Sometimes they think that the orchestra is this incredible sucking hole of red ink. That's why there are very few ballet orchestras left in this country. The first thing a ballet company does to save money is to cut the orchestra." Boston has cut its orchestra considerably in recent years. Even if there's an orchestra for performances, McPhee is alarmed by choreographers who work to recordings in rehearsals instead of to live music, i.e., a pianist who can work with the choreographer or répétiteur on the subtleties of marrying dance and music. "Dancers get the flow of the movement through the body in rehearsal," McPhee says, "and if they rehearse to recorded music, it doesn't go with the live music in performance. It's parallel. I find that, more and more, dance suffers from not being rehearsed to live music."

Making matters even more challenging, there are inevitable tensions between musicians and dancers and their respective unions. Dancers in Boston Ballet work with one-year contracts and don't know from one year to the next if they'll be rehired. Generally their careers are over by the time they're 35 or so. The musicians in the Boston Ballet Orchestra work under a tenure system not unlike that in academia. They can perform until they're 65 if they want to. And they earn more money per hour than the dancers do. However, the musicians don't work as many hours as the dancers do.

In the early 1990s the musicians union agreed that Boston Ballet could perform one program a season without the full orchestra. The choreographers can use taped music, but, says McPhee, "Mikko has made a real commitment to having as many works as possible in that 'taped' program actually be live, maybe a piano solo or a chamber ensemble." Even so, that one program without the orchestra saves the ballet considerable money.

The ballet and its orchestra face, as do other companies worldwide, the legal and logistical issues of CDs, iTunes, DVDs, and videos—the modern means of broadcasting music and dance to a wide public. As of the end of 2007, the CDs sold in the boutique that the Ballet set up when it was in residence at the Wang were *The Nutcracker, Sleeping Beauty, Romeo and Juliet,* and *Holidays in Boston.* "The CD of *The Nutcracker,*" McPhee says proudly, "is the top-selling CD of that ballet in history." The company also has a new agreement with iTunes. "We'll be the first ballet company to be on iTunes. Press *Nutcracker* on iTunes now, and Boston Ballet's recording will pop up. It's a kind of brand-building, a way for the organization to get the word out.

"Up until now I haven't allowed CDs in national distribution," McPhee says. "The way the recording industry works in this country, it's incredibly prohibitive in cost, which is why so many people go to Europe to record. The distribution here is so costly that you don't make any money in the end. I trained as a recording engineer at Juilliard, and I put four years into a business plan for the Ballet. We keep it all in house and sell the CDs only in the ballet boutique, so we keep the retail. People can also go to the Web site and buy them. And Boston Ballet orchestra recordings are played on national radio. In a way, the orchestra has allowed the company to go out across the country." (Of course, Nissinen's goal is to have the dancers go out across the country as well.)

"The real stumbling block," McPhee says, "is putting out a video. CDs are relatively simple. But videos involve cooperation from seven different unions. In the last twenty-five years American ballet has been taped more in Denmark than in the United States because of the union costs here. There are exceptions: *Live from Lincoln Center* is one. Most of *Dance in America* was produced in Denmark. They've got the TV studios set up and an orchestra on salary. But those are one-shot deals. If we had had the ability to bring in professional film crews over the years, we would have had quite the archive."

McPhee says that the Boston Ballet orchestra actually contributes monetarily to the company, through sales of the CDs. That contribution is not enough to cover its expenses, however, and the orchestra isn't allowed to raise funds independently. "I think," McPhee says, not surprisingly, "that anyone who wants to give money to any part of the ballet enterprise should be encouraged."

McPhee and Nissinen have different views about conducting for ballet. Nissinen says that the difference is that "under previous regimes, Jonathan would bend to the wishes of the dancers in terms of tempi. I'm the opposite. I say to the dancers, 'Open your ears and dance the way the music was written.'"

The problem comes in defining the way the music was written. "You take five recordings of Beethoven's Fifth," McPhee says, "and you'll get five completely different experiences. In a Petipa ballet like *Sleeping Beauty*, if you have three different Auroras dancing the traditional variations, you'll get three slightly different versions of the music."

There's more musical leeway in a solo, of course, than in a corps de ballet of twenty-four women, where each woman doesn't get a say about what the tempo should be. In a legendary solo such as *The Dying Swan*, ballerinas have strong opinions about how the music should be played and the dance presented. A dancer who is expected to pour out her heart and focus completely can't do so if she's at odds with the pace of the music. "The choreography for *The Dying Swan* is so incredibly locked to the music," McPhee says. "How the dancer moves is going to affect how the cellist moves. The cellist and harpist can't see the stage at all, of course. The conductor is what holds the piece together. I did it once with Maya Plisetskaya. She was so clear about the music. It was as if she was the cellist, who just happened to have on a white outfit."

Of course, there are times when every dancer has to have the same take on the music. In the spring of 2006 the company was rehearsing part of Petipa's *Raymonda* for "An Evening of Russian Dance." There is a famous moment when four men face the audience and, one at a time, each executes a double tour en l'air, a straight up and down jump starting and ending with feet crossed in fifth position. While airborne, the dancer turns two full revolutions. Any deviation from perfect straightness or any wobbling on landing kills the effect. The musical issue is whether the dancers take off on the beat or come down on it. They all have to do the same thing, and the Boston dancers didn't know which it was. At one point during a rehearsal soloist Jared Redick turned to McPhee and said in frustration, "I'm following you, and you're following me following the beat." Or there are too many followers and no one to lead. McPhee says that the decision about jumping or landing on the count is made by the stager, in this case Nissinen, who was in the room. The answer wasn't in his head. But, from long experience with the choreography, it was certainly in his muscles. So he got up and demonstrated the step. The answer turned out to be to land on the beat.

Perhaps the least traditional choreographer McPhee deals with at Boston Ballet is Jorma Elo. How does McPhee feel about the way Elo works with music? "That's a volatile question. He's incredibly talented, but he's still in process. I asked him right before rehearsals were going to start what music he was using for *Plan to B,* which was premiered in 2004 and reprised in 2006. He had the music, but he had no clue what it was. He had gotten some CD and downloaded it into his laptop. We listened to it and had to guess what it was." (It turned out to be by the seventeenth-century composer Heinrich Ignaz Franz von Biber.)

"Choreographers have so much available on recordings," McPhee says. "It's an incredible advantage to them, with iTunes and Rhapsody." The way Elo works with music comes partly from his many years with Jiři Kylián's Nederlands Dans Theater. "For the last twenty years NDT has been a taped company. That influences what goes on. Elo deconstructs dance, and he does it with music, too. He cuts things up and adds them to the soundscape."

Elo's *Carmen,* which Boston Ballet premiered in 2006, "was different because we knew he was going to use the Shchedrin score." (Rodion

Shchedrin is a Russian composer married to the ballerina Maya Plisetskaya. He reworked the original Bizet score for *Carmen*.) "My own personal feeling," says McPhee, "is that you shouldn't do a ballet at all to *Carmen*. Choreography requires large phrases for movement. *Carmen*, the opera, doesn't have long phrases. It's a couple of bars and then a vocal flourish. It's the opposite of what you need for a ballet. Shchedrin recognized that and re-created it for dance."

The beginning of McPhee's career coincided with the decline of Rudolf Nureyev's. "I was contracted to do his tempi. I called it paint-by-numbers. My job was to make him look good, to make the performances work with the physical limitations he had then. Musically it's not very satisfying to do that. I did it, but I didn't do it any more with him. He asked me to go on a solo tour with him, and I declined. The difficulty is that some people in the ballet world would look at that comment and become incensed, because Nureyev was such an idol to them." Superstar status doesn't come with a lifetime guarantee, but audiences are reluctant to recognize that. Often they're clapping for what they saw or heard twenty years ago. "The last time I heard Pavarotti, it was terrible," McPhee says, "but the audience went crazy anyhow."

McPhee talked about the rather convoluted path that, after conducting for the best dance companies in the world, eventually brought him to Boston. "The roots of my career are in my studies at the Royal Academy of Music in London in the 1970s. Students at the RAM got free tickets to the Royal Ballet." So in the 1970s McPhee regularly saw such glorious dancers as Antoinette Sibley and Anthony Dowell. (Later in his career, McPhee would conduct Sibley's last performance.) His teacher at RAM encouraged him to take ballet lessons. "I'd been a gymnast at school, so I had an inkling of what was involved." He took the classes until "I was thrown out of England. The Labor government came in, and I got this notice that I could work there temporarily, but after graduating I'd have to become a British citizen in order to stay. I hadn't intended to leave England, but I went home to Buffalo, where I continued ballet classes. There was this whole dead year after the Royal Academy. It was scary, because I didn't know what would happen." What happened was that he got into Juilliard, where he earned two degrees. "The night I conducted my last performance at Juilliard, a little note came floating backstage. It said, 'Loved the performance. Call me.' And it had her home phone number." The note was from Martha Graham. Soon McPhee was Graham's second conductor, then her principal one. "She said the thing that impressed her was my breathing, that the way they breathe is what dancers and musicians have in common."

During McPhee's first gig with Graham, the tour ended with six weeks at the Metropolitan Opera House, where he met the famous friends who supported the Graham company, including Nureyev and Liza Minnelli. "Halston would be running around backstage," McPhee recalls. "He turned out to be a good friend to me and an even better one to Graham. They were really close. Every time Graham had a deficit, Halston wrote a check. I used to do all the music budgets for the New York seasons. 'I don't care what it costs,' he would say. 'Martha will always exist.' Mr. Balanchine came to the Graham season and said, 'Would you like to conduct *Nutcracker* next month?'" The answer was yes. "Then Mr. Joffrey came by and offered me full-time employment. The Joffrey Ballet became my home company for six years. It was the golden age of dance in New York, the 1980s." When he wasn't working for the Joffrey Ballet, McPhee was still a guest conductor for companies including American Ballet Theatre and New York City Ballet. He wisely got, and has kept, glowing letters of recommendations from the likes of Graham and Leonard Bernstein. "Then the AIDS thing decimated the world of dance. I still don't think we've recovered."

McPhee came to Boston in the late 1980s, burned out from touring. "Thirty-six weeks a year of living out of your suitcase," he says, "that's hard." Besides, he and his wife were starting a family, and "New York isn't a good place to raise children." An invitation from Bruce Marks, then Boston Ballet's artistic director, came out of the blue. Would McPhee want to conduct a contemporary festival? He would, although with some reservations. "The music was all over the map. The rehearsal time was ridiculously short. I looked at the dancers and said, 'This is not up to what I'm used to.' Boston Ballet was the least developed company I had ever worked with. Most importantly, I met the orchestra, which was full of potential but had just come off a strike. Relations between the orchestra and the company weren't good. But I looked at the potential of their working together, and that's what made me sign on.

"Technically and artistically at first the company wasn't at the level I had been working with. Now they are. I don't think they get half the credit they deserve. The community doesn't realize what it's got. It kills me that Mikko isn't able to do what he wants, to push his audiences and his dancers. I have no regrets about moving to Boston," McPhee says, "but I'm glad to have done what I did before I came. When we get on the stage, making music and dancing and connecting with the audience are the only things that count."

McPhee has studied the notebooks of Serge Diaghilev, the great Russian impresario who introduced the Ballets Russes to Europe early in the twentieth century. Diaghilev was chronically one step ahead of his creditors. (His finances make Boston Ballet's look healthy.) Making matters more difficult, he was working in the era of the Russian Revolution and World War I. But his name has become synonymous with pioneering art, with choreography by Fokine, Nijinska, Nijinsky, and Balanchine, music by the likes of Stravinsky, and décor by Picasso and Matisse. "It's amazing the crushing challenges that he learned to cope with," says McPhee. "All we remember now are the glories of the Ballets Russes." He's implicitly saying that the legacy of Boston Ballet will be in its exciting choreography, not its financial problems.

"The last seven years in Boston have been some of the most difficult and instructive in my life," he says. "It's partly the turmoil the company has gone through and the difficulty of raising money in Yankee territory." The board had such faith not only in McPhee's capabilities as a conductor but also in his knowledge of how a ballet company works that in the rudderless year between Gielgud's departure and Nissinen's arrival on a full-time basis, McPhee was named interim artistic coordinator, the senior artistic staff member in the absence of an artistic director.

He is a regular presence at rehearsals, usually standing beside Freda Locker, the company's principal pianist and an important figure in the organization. "Good ballet pianists are harder and harder to find," says McPhee. "The piano reductions of ballet scores are handwritten, and some are 100 years old. They're terribly difficult to read. You would think that after all these years, the piano reductions would be clean. But even at New York City Ballet they're not. A lot of pianists pick up what they play from the orchestra. That's usually the most successful way to deal with the problem."

Freda Locker

Locker's résumé is as short and simple as McPhee's is dense. It doesn't even fill a single sheet of paper, double spaced. She grew up in a big family in Pittsburgh. Her mother was a piano teacher but didn't believe in teaching her own children (which could have emotional results like those that so often occur when a parent tries to teach a child to drive). With six siblings all taking piano lessons from other teachers but practicing on the 1927 Steinway at home, "things got pretty noisy at times," she says. Locker studied ballet, too. "But I didn't have the talent to pursue it." She does, however, know the steps and what tempo each requires, which is particularly necessary when playing for company classes. Class is a collaboration not only between teacher and dancers but also with the accompanist. What to play is an issue. "The ballet teacher sets the meter and the length," Locker says. "You can't play Stravinsky for a class, because everything has to come out even. There are books on ballet class music. I've used them lots because I have trouble with improvisation. Some teachers, including Mikko, don't want us to play ballet music because the dancers are so sick of the stuff." (There are tales of ballet dancers stuck in elevators in July and weeping as *Nutcracker* music is piped in.)

Perhaps the greatest musical challenge of the spring 2006 season was *Les Noces.* McPhee describes Bronislava Nijinska's 1923 masterwork as

Freda Locker accompanying a rehearsal. Photo by Wally Gilbert.

"one of those pieces that sits in a crack. I've never really understood why until we did this production. People think of *Le Sacre du Printemps* as the thing that Stravinsky did during this period beyond which he could go no further." The legendary booing and rioting at the 1913 premiere of *Le Sacre du Printemps,* choreographed by Nijinska's brother, Vaslav Nijinsky, has tended to overshadow *Les Noces.* Nijinska couldn't make sense of the score, says McPhee. Stravinsky himself had to play for rehearsals.

"I've never seen a good performance of it," McPhee said before the Boston premiere. The stager in Boston was Aleth Francillon, a former ballet mistress at the Paris Opera Ballet. "She brought a DVD of *Les Noces* with her from the Paris Opera. It was a mess," McPhee says. "When Stravinsky composed it, he went through three different orchestrations. He did one for a massive orchestra, and then one for mechanical instruments, but he couldn't program them to stay together." (Today, of course, he would be able to.) "Then he landed on the idea of four pianos and percussion. It was right. Lean." Francillon keyed off the piano reduction, which, McPhee says, "in this case was a kind of shorthand of what Stravinsky did. Most of the stuff was in his head, while he was playing a little bit of it on the piano. It's part of an aural history of playing something that's not on the page. Things weren't written down. We had to start from scratch, putting together our own hybrid reduction. I brought in another pianist and piano and picked through the score. Freddy and Francillon and I figured out what this new reduction would be. Francillon knew the steps inside out. But she had always been doing them to a reduction that didn't match, because of the history of handing things down person to person rather than writing them clearly in the beginning. At the end, Francillon recognized what we had done. She said we had done it better than any other production she had seen. It's like doing a Balanchine ballet. If you don't find his understanding of the music, it's a disaster. The choreography and the music in *Les Noces* are so integrated. She needed to hear things that weren't in that one piano reduction." Lloyd Schwartz, the Pulitzer Prize–winning music critic for the *Boston Phoenix,* said he hadn't been aware of the three different orchestrations, but he pronounced Boston's performance of *Les Noces* "truly impressive." McPhee, meanwhile, presented Francillon with a copy of the new score, which was, he says, "what she had needed all along."

13

The Design Team

Costumes

Charles K. Heightchew is Boston Ballet's wardrobe manager, in charge of a staff of about fifteen with titles that include wigmaster, wig and makeup artists, draper, and stitcher. He's not only in charge of the costume shop but is also beginning to design costumes himself. He seems perfectly suited to his role. Raised and schooled in Louisville, Kentucky, he had a mother who taught him how to sew, a subscription to the Louisville Ballet, and a degree in art history from the University of Louisville. "The Louisville Ballet was filled with good, strong dancers," he recalls. "But they were short. I saw Dance Theatre of Harlem on tour and thought, 'Wow! What a different body type!'" That difference got him thinking about making costumes for ballet.

He's also worked in costume shops in summer stock, children's theater, and opera companies. His first job at Boston Ballet was as a draper, a job he explains as "translating a two-dimensional design on paper into muslin mock-ups that solve the issues of the dancer's proportions and shape. You get all that worked out before you make the real thing. For tutus there's a basic recipe: we make four smalls, fifteen mediums, etc. We can skip the muslin stage there."

It takes two to six fittings for each garment, and several dancers must fit into the same costume for financial reasons. (In better funded European companies, each ballerina has her own tutu for each role.) The fitting is somewhat easier than it might seem, because tutus, although they look like one garment onstage, are actually two: each has a separate bodice and skirt. So Heightchew can switch around bodices and skirts to suit the individual dancer's figure. "Some girls have wider backs, and some have wider ribs. I average $1,200 for a new tutu and bodice when I'm costing things out. A typical tutu has nine to thirteen layers of tulle, depending on the desired 'look' of the particular ballet. The netting is relatively inexpensive. The layers are sewn on by machine, except for the top one, which is stitched by hand. You can spend 79 cents a yard for the netting, but the garment won't hold up. If you use $5 a yard netting, the result can last fifteen years." The tutu storage in Heightchew's basement wardrobe room makes visitors smile or even giggle: the skirts are slid one after the other onto upright iron poles. They look like a stack of doughnuts—but they stay fluffy. Folding a tutu would take away its signature platterlike shape.

Male costumes are easier. The bottoms are generally elasticized tights that come in standard sizes.

"In 2006 the most complex costumes were for *Carmen,*" Heightchew says. "And there were around 200 of them. The designer, Joke Visser, made samples for us to follow. The women wore short organza skirts. It's not all black and red, as *Carmen*s usually are. We had 225 yards of fabric dyed to make them." Sometimes Heightchew has to outsource costumes because his staff isn't large enough to make them in a sufficient quantity for a production as big as *Carmen.* So the men's suits were made in Atlanta out of silk-satin because, Heightchew says, "Jorma Elo really likes shiny fabrics." They're not stretch cloth. They're all tailored to fit the choreography so they won't rip."

Part of Heightchew's job is watching rehearsals to see how the costumes fit the dancers and how well they move with the choreography. The costumes for *Raymonda* are almost twenty years old, but they're original to Boston Ballet, so Heightchew has had plenty of time to remake large parts of them. Watching Karine Seneca in a rehearsal of the pas de deux that is *Raymonda*'s culmination, he winces slightly as her bodice is awkwardly scrunched in a lift, and he fixes the problem when the duet is over. He tries to catch all these little glitches before the curtain goes up on the real performance.

For each season's costumes, "We start with the repertory Mikko chooses, and then we create a budget," says Heightchew, who still keeps his hand in opera and generally does one opera production a year. He contrasts making opera costumes with those for ballet. "You get much

longer-range planning in opera. The singers know what they're doing three or four years ahead of time. Dancers don't. Last year I had to make guesses about who would have the leading roles in Boston Ballet after I learned what the rep was."

Tutu and bodice for *Raymonda,* act 3. Photo by Wally Gilbert.

The costumes for the new work that Mark Morris made for the company in 2006, *Up and Down,* "look like simple street wear but aren't. Each of those little dresses had to have a built-in bra, which meant a lot of hand-stitching."

In the spring 2007 season, the most lavish costumes were those for Balanchine's *A Midsummer Night's Dream,* designed by Martin Pakledinaz for the ballet's premiere in 1962 and subsequently remade or refurbished as needed. These particular *Midsummer* costumes were on loan from Pacific Northwest Ballet. Hanging in the small storage space Heightchew has behind his office (space is so tight that most costumes are stored off the premises) are racks of *Midsummer* costumes so exquisitely made that they could be the product of an old-school haute couture house. Seams are reinforced. Faux jewels are sewn onto the bodices by hand. Fabrics are sumptuous. One look at these gorgeous garments puts paid to the stereotype of Balanchine preferring plain leotards and tights as costumes. He used them when money was scarce and also when leotards would show off the choreography better than something voluminous. But he loved elaborate costumes, too.

Heightchew researches historical costumes, and he's in a good part of the country for it, with the Harvard Theatre Collection in Cambridge and the Wadsworth Atheneum in Hartford, both with rich collections of historic costumes, particularly from the Diaghilev era.

Some of Natalia Gontcharova's designs for Bronislava Nijinska's 1923 *Les Noces* are in the collections of the Wadsworth, so Heightchew made a field trip to Hartford when he learned that Boston would be doing the ballet. The costumes are as revolutionary as the choreography. Both men and women wear long white peasant shirts. The women's heads are wrapped—almost bandaged—in white, and they wear dark, loose shifts

Dancer's makeup table with wig. Photo by Wally Gilbert.

that conceal the shape of the body beneath. Nothing could be further from a tight-fitting sequined tutu bodice. Heightchew wanted to stay true to the original, so he used the fabrics of the 1923 production—wool crepe and crinkle cotton—to create the right textures.

"Each new set of costumes inevitably speaks of its own age," Heightchew says. "Before stretch fabrics, before Lycra and Spandex, costumes were entirely different." Hence those early photographs of dancers wearing silk tights sagging at the knees.

Pointe Shoes

Kathleen Mitchell's cramped, airless basement headquarters, next to Heightchew's space, doesn't reflect the importance of her role. Shoes are a make or break factor for dancers. If a ballerina's pointe shoes don't fit correctly, her performance can be a disaster. Mitchell knows that well. She was a professional dancer herself, with San Francisco Ballet, and then she was San Francisco's toe shoe manager before taking the same position in Boston.

"I got into managing shoes in San Francisco because I had spent thirty years wearing them," she says. "I learned that they should be part of your foot rather than an appendage. You don't want the audience to be conscious of the shoes. They should disappear, so people just see the performance." So shoes are dyed to fit the palette of a particular ballet. For Jorma Elo's *Carmen,* for instance, the toe shoes were covered either with shoe spray or pancake makeup to make the feet indistinguishable from the leg.

There was no Big Bang resulting in the invention of the pointe shoe, and several dancers performed on the tips of their toes in the early 1800s, although as a sort of novelty. By the 1830s, Marie Taglioni, one of the great ballerinas of her age, was dancing on pointe in ballets choreographed by her father, Filippo. The Taglionis transformed pointe work into a means of expression in what's come to be called the Romantic ballet. Among the most famous examples of the genre, and one of the earliest, is *La Sylphide,* which premiered at the Paris Opera, headquarters for the Romantic ballet movement, in 1832, with choreography by Filippo and starring Marie. It's not this version but the 1836 one by August Bournonville that has come down to us. Boston's version of *La Sylphide* is credited to Sorella Englund, "after August Bournonville."

The pointe shoe was the perfect vehicle for suggesting supernatural beings—ghosts, sylphs, wilis, and such—and enabled the ballerina to create the illusion of floating across the stage in the tiny steps called bourrées. By the end of the nineteenth century, though, pointe work had become a gimmick in the service of technical feats such as the thirty-two fouetté turns that the ballerina performs in *Swan Lake*. By the beginning of the twentieth century, ballet choreographers such as Fokine, Nijinsky, and Nijinska were rejecting the automatic use of pointe work, incorporating it only when it suited the theme of a ballet. By the end of the century, modern dance choreographers including Twyla Tharp and Mark Morris were experimenting with pointe work.

Early pointe shoes were soft ballet slippers darned at the tips to make them stiff. Gradually they evolved into the shoes of today, made of layers of canvas, glue, Hessian (a form of burlap), and satin, with the shank of the shoe made of leather. "They're all organic materials," says Mitchell, "which allows the shoes to be soundless." (In theory, at least. Many is the ballet-goer who has shivered at the clunking sound of a swan's crash landing.)

Tying on pointe shoes. Photo by Wally Gilbert.

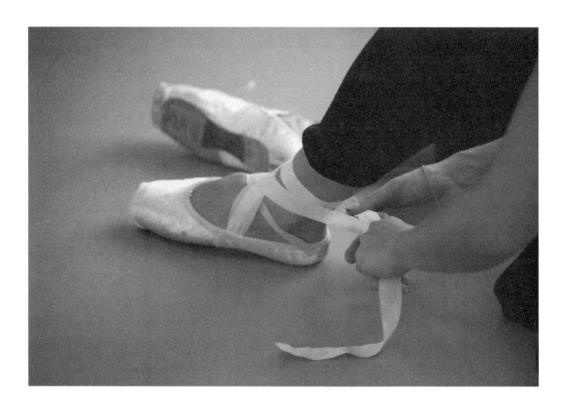

The organic nature of the materials is also, alas, appealing to insects and rodents known to nosh on toe shoes. So in Boston Ballet's basement shoe room, the footwear is sealed in red plastic bins, one for each dancer in the company. Ballet dancers have more shoes than Imelda Marcos ever dreamed of, the difference being that dancers go through one pair at a time.

"For each female dancer I place an initial order of seventy pairs for the entire season, from August through May," Mitchell says, "and they get one pair per week of layoff. There are dancers who use fewer pairs and dancers who use twice as many." At retail, shoes cost $80 a pair. The company gets a hefty discount. Male dancers, who don't wear pointe shoes, are allocated fifteen pairs of soft slippers a year.

"It can take from three to eleven months to get an order made," explains Mitchell, who always has to be thinking ahead. "You have to get in your maker's queue, and dancers switching companies may lose their place in the queue and spend an entire year getting it back. My biggest nightmare is a dancer running out of shoes."

Most dancers in Boston Ballet wear shoes by one of the field's two

Autographed pointe shoes waiting to be sold. Photo by Wally Gilbert.

biggest manufacturers, Freed and Bloch. Representatives from Freed visit Boston Ballet twice a year for marathon measuring sessions for both professional dancers and students. Once their measurements are in the system, students can order their shoes online. The shoes worn by students aren't subsidized by the company, and the cost can be considerable. Company general manager David Tompkins, whose wife and her two sisters were both involved in ballet, remembers the family story of his father-in-law coming into a room with a garbage bag filled with worn toe shoes, emptying them onto the floor, and saying to his daughters, "There. Those are your scholarships."

Traditionally, the shoes are all made by men. Mitchell makes them sound like the little old shoemakers of fairytale fame. "They all have nicknames," she says. "My maker was Upside Down Triangle, which was how he signed my shoes." Some other makers' names sound like British pubs. Key, Crown, and Bell are a few she mentions.

For a ballet dancer, a visit to Mitchell's headquarters is just the beginning of her relationship with her new shoes, a relationship that culminates with rubbing the bottoms of toe shoes in a box of powdered rosin, a traction aid and generally one of the last things a dancer does before setting foot onstage.

But before that, she tortures her shoes to break them in. Some dancers shut the pristine pink satin slippers in a door jamb. Others beat them against the floor. Some glue on suede tips for better traction. Some use a tool called a rasper, which has metal teeth, to scrape the bottoms of the shoes, the better to hold the rosin. Spraying shellac on the shoes helps make them last longer, as does darning the tips. To make the shoes easier on the foot, many dancers use a bit of padding, once lamb's wool but now anything from paper towels to sock ends, inside the shoes. Less is considered more in this area: dancers want to "feel" the floor the way the driver of a sports car wants to "feel" the road. Even the most exalted ballerinas sew their own ribbons and elastics onto their shoes. Placement of these essentials for holding the shoe on the foot is a very personal matter, not to be entrusted to anyone else.

Boston Ballet's shoe budget is $150,000 a season. "Pro basketball players can go through a pair of shoes each game," Mitchell says with a touch of envy. "They can afford to, because of endorsement contracts. You don't see a Nike swoosh on a toe shoe." The expense of toe shoes has

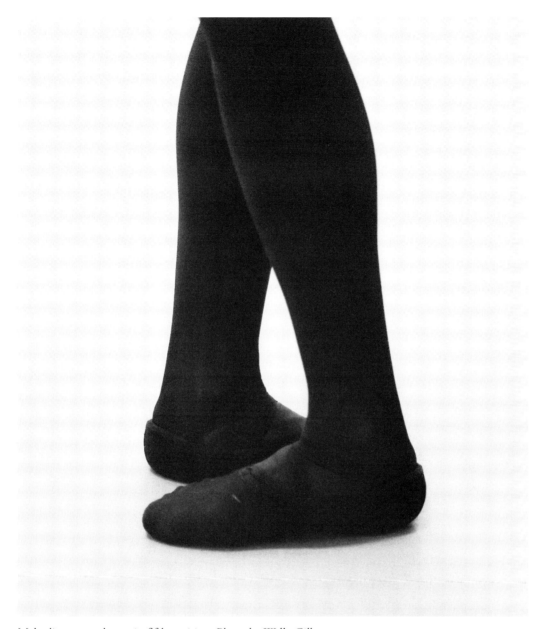

Male slippers on dancer in fifth position. Photo by Wally Gilbert.

led companies, including Boston's, to recycle them. Dancers autograph their "dead" shoes, which are then sent to the boutique that the Boston Ballet sets up in the theater lobby, to be sold as souvenirs. Principals' and soloists' old shoes go for $40 a pair, and corps dancers' sell for $15.

Sets

As for ballet sets, the general mandate is to leave as much of the stage as clear as possible, maximizing the space for dancing. Portability is also important. A relatively compact, lightweight backdrop is easier to take on tour than something large and unwieldy. Sets for ballet are expensive, and many companies rent sets to one another to amortize the upfront cost. "Mikko generally wants new sets for new choreography," says David Tompkins, "but he'll also rent other ones from other companies. Sometimes the rent is so exorbitant that we end up building our own anyway. If you're doing a popular ballet like *Romeo and Juliet,* there's also a good chance that other companies will want to hire those sets. Our *Sleeping Beauty* production is particularly popular: we bought it from the Royal Ballet."

Like most companies, Boston Ballet doesn't have an in-house set designer but hires designers whose style fits the theme of the ballet and the taste of the choreographer and artistic director. In the 2006–07 Boston Ballet season, the set most unlike the typical forest-in-the-background of *La Sylphide* or *Giselle* was that for Jorma Elo's *Carmen.* Elo himself worked on the sets, along with designer Walt Spangler. Because Elo has updated his *Carmen* so that the women are supermodels and the men are hip businessmen or race car drivers, the set consists of a runway on which the expressionless models sway their hips while selling clothing (and possibly themselves) and a large pair of gray metal curves that open and close to suit whatever the scene requires. Lit from the back you can see through them, but if lit from the front they become an impenetrable wall. In such cases, with scenery that takes a part of the action, the choreographer and designer must work closely together.

Elo's lighting effects are also notably dramatic, and he's as involved with them as he is with his sets. He thinks up the basic ideas before handing them on to professionals who realize them. The lighting designer in *Carmen* was Mikki Kunttu, who created effects as spectacular as a lightning storm.

The Production Department, under production manager/technical director Benjamin Phillips, must ensure that such imaginative creations meet the demands of real performances. Phillips has designed works for Elo and others. His staff includes production stage manager

Craig Margolis, a lighting electrician, a sound engineer, and a lighting programmer.

Sometimes unfamiliar sets are already in situ when a touring company arrives in town. Woe to the dancers who fail to check them out before performing with them. In her 1977 book, *Giselle: A Role for a Lifetime*, Violette Verdy, former New York City Ballet star and erstwhile Boston Ballet director, offers some practical tips. When touring in *Giselle,* she writes, she always checked the door of the cottage where Giselle and her mother live. Does it open in or out? She mentions a ballerina friend who once missed an entrance because she wrestled with getting the sticky door to open at all, making the entire cottage shake as she did so.

The size of the stage is critical, especially in such works as the big Tchaikovsky ballets: *Swan Lake, Sleeping Beauty,* and *The Nutcracker.* From the first time Boston Ballet performed *Nutcracker* in the Opera House it was obvious that the stage couldn't accommodate all elements of the huge, elaborate sets designed especially for the Wang. So a lot of the decor stayed in storage. And, Nissinen says, "If we used our complete *Swan Lake* sets in the Opera House, they would look squashed."

14

The Critics

Do dance critics make a difference? In Boston, there are still two daily newspapers, the *Boston Globe* and the *Boston Herald,* and a significant weekly, the *Boston Phoenix.* Those are the publications that count most to Boston Ballet's administration, its dancers, and its public. On the administrative side there is hope that a good review will sell tickets, and because the Ballet generally performs each program for just one or two weeks (a "week" actually being a long weekend, running from Thursday through Sunday), it must sell them fast if they're being bought on the basis of a review. In terms of ticket sales, preview coverage may be even more important to the company than a review, but previews in Boston have become very rare. As for the dancers, who performs on opening night is particularly important, because usually only the opening night cast will be reviewed.

It's not a given that when Boston Ballet performs something of particular note, critics from New York come to review it. McPhee recalls that he and Nissinen were surprised and disappointed that no New York critic came to review *Les Noces* in the spring of 2006, which, in the version Boston danced, hadn't been performed in New York since 1981.

As is the case in most U.S. cities, no Boston newspaper any longer has a staff dance critic, which means that they rely on freelancers who are typically paid about $150 for a review and must be nimble enough to produce it in an hour or so after the show to meet the deadline. That doesn't leave them much time to ponder a production they might have seen only that one time. They generally support themselves with day jobs that provide real salaries and benefits.

"The attitude of the newspapers in Boston," says David Tompkins, "is 'You did *Swan Lake* a few years ago. We don't need to write about it again.'" He's exaggerating, but things have gotten worse in recent years, both in Boston and in other American cities.

Francia Russell, former codirector of Seattle's Pacific Northwest Ballet, says bluntly, "There never was a dance critic who knew anything about ballet in Seattle." She blames the *New York Times* for its lack of coverage. "They're supposed to be a national newspaper, but they focus primarily on New York."

After Maina Gielgud was appointed director designate of Boston Ballet, she asked local critics whether they were allowed by their publications to review multiple casts of the same ballet. Ten years earlier the answer would have been yes, at least at the city's largest daily, the *Globe.* That's not the case anymore, except at the *Phoenix*, whose arts editor, Jeffrey Gantz, is an enthusiastic balletomane who allows himself the space to write expansive critiques of 1,400 words, covering several casts. Gantz explains his road to reviewing multiple casts. Former *Phoenix* dance critic Laura Jacobs (now writing in New York) "showed up in Boston in the 1980s," he recalls. "I started going to performances with her, and she gave me intelligent information. She was into seeing different casts, and that taught me a lot. You don't get the chance to compare and contrast in many other artistic areas."

Fifteen or twenty years ago, as the staff dance critic at the *Globe,* not only was I allowed to write reviews of multiple casts—I topped out at five *Giselle*s one season—but my colleague Richard Dyer, the *Globe's* classical music critic, was also encouraged to review the music in ballet performances, especially in the case of an exceptionally musical choreographer such as Mark Morris. No longer.

Gantz's knowledge of ballet is, sadly, hindered by his own publication. "I've been to New York to see dance only a few times," he says. Why not more? "The problem is the *Phoenix* won't pay for travel. They don't care what goes on in New York. I'd like to go more, but I'd have to pay for it myself."

For most of the time that I was the dance critic for the *Globe,* 1978–2005, I was allowed to travel not only to New York but all over the country and abroad as well. One year I did a major trip to see and compare the most prominent U.S. companies and write about them. Another year I was sent to cover dance in St. Petersburg, and the *Globe* also sent a staff photographer. I would frequently travel to write previews of ballet companies about to visit Boston. In some purist camps, it's considered bad for the same person to preview and review a performance because a preview is likely to sway the critic's opinion. I disagree. My being allowed to travel meant that more often than not, my previews were in effect pre-reviews. I interviewed choreographers, but I also saw performances in various cities. Other critics in Boston weren't so fortunate. Their previews were often in the form of telephone interviews with choreographers whose work was unfamiliar to them and with dancers whom they had never seen perform.

Back in the days when America's big cities each had several daily newspapers, if one newspaper's critic hated a piece, the critic at another paper might like it. The presence of only one or two critics in a city engenders a sense of responsibility and moderation. The critical response to *Up and Down,* the new work Mark Morris created for Boston Ballet in 2006, brought a disagreement that was refreshing in an era of cautious criticism. Writing in the *Globe,* freelance critic Thea Singer commented that the Morris premiere was "exquisitely proportioned and architecturally sound, while springing straight from the music [by Alexander Glazunov] and hitting you smack in the heart. The pieces by the other artists—Helen Pickett, Jorma Elo, and Val Caniparoli—either fade or don't even make it into the ballpark."

A few days later, commenting on National Public Radio station WBUR's Online Arts Web site, Debra Cash, long a Boston freelancer, opened with her interpretation of Morris's comment that after Balanchine died, people started to believe that everything he had done was great. Morris's point, said Cash, was that "such veneration was a patent absurdity, obscuring actual achievements under the undiscriminating veil of the master's reputation." Cash then accused some critics and fans of adopting a similar "kneejerk partiality" to Morris's work. She went on to declare *Up and Down* "a dud."

Writing about the program in the *New York Times,* which does occasionally cover Boston Ballet, dance critic John Rockwell opened with a flippant description of Morris's curtain call, then a vague description of the actual choreography, with the only detailed comment on "the sour playing of the four saxophonists who manhandled Glazunov's quirky Quartet." Rockwell was far better known as a music critic than a dance writer, and after his retirement he was replaced at the *Times* by a well qualified British critic, Alastair Macaulay.

Iris Fanger, who has written about Boston Ballet over the years for the *Boston Globe,* the *Christian Science Monitor,* and many local publications, recalls, "I always had lots of space in the newspapers." In 2006 and 2007, the *Patriot Ledger,* a literate suburban daily, allowed Fanger 600–850 words, which is more than the *Globe* usually allows now.

"With the *Globe* having no staff dance critic any more," Gantz says, "it's sending a bad message. They have stringers, but some of the stuff they publish is pretty poor. You have to cultivate critics by creating over time someone that people will read, listen to, and maybe argue with. That takes time to build up. You can't do it with stringers, and you can't do it with someone who has never seen much of anything. Without that support, I don't think that reviews have much impact."

Marcia B. Siegel has written dance criticism for over forty years in New York and Boston. For the last eleven years she's been a freelancer for the *Phoenix.* There has been friction between Siegel and Gantz over who covers what. Gantz reviews Boston Ballet, but Siegel says, "If I'm the dance critic, I have to do the ballet as well as the modern dance. If Jeffrey wants to do it also, as a critic-at-large, fine. When my stuff is not on the Web, I don't even know if it's in print. They don't own it, though. I hold the copyright."

The *Globe* lost Debra Cash as a critic after the paper demanded that all freelancers sign a contract ceding all rights, including future rights in all media, to their work for the paper. Cash moved to WBUR Online Arts, which was axed in 2006 because, the radio station announced, its main mission was news and analysis, not arts.

The problem is hardly unique to Boston. After serving as the dance critic at the *Village Voice* in New York for forty years, Deborah Jowitt was laid off in 2008.

Cash no longer has a regular place to publish. "Dance criticism has, in general, dried up," she says. "We've got a situation where there are universities granting degrees to students to prepare them to be critics. But there aren't any jobs. So they develop blogs. But blogs don't pay."

Lorna Feijóo in *La Sylphide* at the Auditorio Conde Duque in Madrid. Photo by Wally Gilbert.

The company in
George Balanchine's
The Four Tempera-
ments, choreography
by George Balanchine,
© The George Balan-
chine Trust, at the
Auditorio Conde
Duque in Madrid.
Photo by Wally
Gilbert.

Melissa Hough, John Lam, and Tempe Ostergren in George Balanchine's *The Four Temperaments*, choreography by George Balanchine, © The George Balanchine Trust, at the Auditorio Conde Duque in Madrid. Photo by Wally Gilbert.

The company in George Balanchine's *Serenade*, choreography by George Balanchine, © The George Balanchine Trust, at the Citi Performing Arts Center Wang Theatre. Photo by Wally Gilbert.

Larissa Ponomarenko rehearsing George Balanchine's *Serenade*, choreography by George Balanchine, © The George Balanchine Trust, at the Auditorio Conde Duque in Madrid. Photo by Wally Gilbert.

Larissa Ponoma-
renko and Pavel
Gurevich rehears-
ing George Bal-
anchine's *Serenade*,
choreography by
George Balanchine,
© The George
Balanchine Trust,
at the Auditorio
Conde Duque in
Madrid. Photo by
Wally Gilbert.

Lorna Feijóo and
Tai Jimenez in
George Balanchine's
Serenade, choreog-
raphy by George
Balanchine, © The
George Balanchine
Trust, at the Citi
Performing Arts
Center Wang The-
atre. Photo by Wally
Gilbert.

Jorma Elo choreo-
graphing *Carmen*
with Sabi Varga.
Photo by Wally
Gilbert.

Karine Seneca and
Carlos Molina
in *Carmen* at the
Citi Performing
Arts Center Wang
Theatre. Photo by
Wally Gilbert.

Bradley Schlagheck
and John Lam
in *Carmen* at the
Citi Performing
Arts Center Wang
Theatre. Photo by
Wally Gilbert.

Lia Cirio and Roman
Rykine in *Carmen* at
the Citi Performing
Arts Center Wang
Theatre. Photo by
Wally Gilbert.

Helen Pickett
teaching Amaker
Smith in a Sum-
mer Dance Pro-
gram class. Photo
by Wally Gilbert.

Heather Myers,
dancer and
choreographer, at
a rehearsal. Photo
by Wally Gilbert.

Kelley Potter and
the Dancing Bear
in *The Nutcracker* at
the Boston Opera
House, reproduced
courtesy of Live
Nation, Inc. Photo
by Wally Gilbert.

The Nutcracker and the Mouse tearing apart the Gingerbread Doll in *The Nutcracker* at the Boston Opera House, reproduced courtesy of Live Nation, Inc. Photo by Wally Gilbert.

Tying pointe shoes. Photo by Wally Gilbert.

PART TWO

The Dancing

15

Auditions

It's a chilly day in early spring of 2007 when young dancers from all over the United States, along with their peers from France, Mexico, Australia, Poland, China, Italy, Venezuela, Brazil, Canada, and Japan, gather in Boston Ballet's building to audition for the company and Boston Ballet II, its apprentice group. There are 100 eager prospects in all, with the 11 Japanese forming the biggest foreign contingent. They've read about the auditions in dance publications or online, or simply heard by word of mouth.

This is an open audition, which means anyone can show up, even a 200-pound 50-year-old. But the group is self-selected. Their teachers or company directors back home will have advised them whether they're ready to try out for a major company. In the past, Nissinen has also held auditions in other cities in America and Europe, with a typical total of 500 dancers trying out each year. The reason he's cut back on that schedule is that the company's finances mean he's not looking for many more dancers. He can't afford them, but also he's building his company primarily from within the ranks. Still, Nissinen sometimes serves as a judge at international ballet competitions that directors trawl to find new company members. And in the course of a year, about 150 dancers send him DVDs of themselves performing. If he likes what he sees, he'll invite them to take company class.

Before this particular audition, the hopeful dancers fill out forms with their contact and training information, then line up to get a number on a big piece of white paper that they pin to their leotards or T-shirts. For today, they're not "David" or "Jane," just "36" or "92."

The 100 dancers have been divided into two groups, with the second group sent to another studio to prepare for their turn and the remaining contenders warming up on the floor in the Grand Studio. At the last minute a ballet administrator decides that the group in the Grand Studio is too big, and he sends 20 of them down to the other studio. They have been preparing to start their audition at 10:45, and now they'll have to wait another hour and a half, which is like taking a race horse out of the starting gate at the last minute, just when it is raring to run. The majority of those auditioning, by far, are young women. There is but one African-American, a man.

Nissinen addresses the first group. "We'll try to make the audition process as easy as possible. All we want to see is good, clean, simple dancing. We realize it's a bit stressful." Then Tamara King, a principal of the Boston Ballet School, pitches the school's five-week intensive summer program for dancers, whose ages ranged from 15 to 23 in 2007. The mutual understanding here is that those who don't make it into the company might come to the school, where the Ballet's artistic staff can take a longer look at them, assessing their promise. The summer program has its own set of auditions, coast-to-coast, to select a predetermined number of students—300 young women and 50 young men. The small number of men is because the school's faculty realizes there just aren't that many male students out there who are sufficiently well trained to qualify for the summer school. (Unlike the Marines, looking for a few good men, the ballet world is still looking for lots of them. The shortage is chronic. As an inducement to come to Boston for the summer, 95 percent of the men chosen for the program are on scholarship.)

The audition begins. It takes the form of a routine class given by Pino Alosa, an Italian ballet master for the company who also works worldwide. The only difference between the audition class and the ones the dancers take daily is that Alosa doesn't offer any corrections. There's no actual instruction. The dancers are there to show what they've already learned. Some want so badly to be noticed that they've claimed prominent spaces at the portable barres that fill the center of the room. Others head for the stationary barres on the walls, less noticeable positions. By the end of the opening exercises they have taken off the warm-up layers, leggings, sweaters, and sweat suits, stripping down to leotards and tights in order to present the best view of their bodies to the rather intimidating half dozen members of the Ballet's artistic staff who sit at the front of the room, taking notes and whispering to each other. It's sadly obvious that a great many of these young people who have devoted five or ten years and often many thousands of their parents' dollars to rigorous training have the "wrong" body type for professional ballet. Their legs or their necks are too short; their heads are too big; or their turnout—the rotation of the legs out from the hip socket—is insufficient.

Today's ballet directors expect dancers to have the elegance of models and the technique of Olympic athletes. In the past, that wasn't necessarily the case. Margot Fonteyn had famously weak feet, and Nijinsky had extremely chunky thighs, but those "flaws" didn't prevent them from becoming dance legends. You wonder what their careers would be like if they were starting out now.

Some of the dancers in the audition are excellent jumpers; others are more proficient in turning. Almost none can land a double pirouette with panache, and that's critical. It's not how many revolutions you can spin around that the audience ultimately remembers.

Style is a factor in the auditions as well. Alosa gives the dancers the gestures of the legs and feet, but he doesn't say anything about heads or arms. The more polished dancers automatically coordinate their heads and arms with the leg movements, making those movements less robotic and more artistic.

After an hour, Nissinen calls out the numbers of those dancers he wants to stay. One by one, the rest of them approach the artistic staff to thank them. The young women curtsy, and the men nod their heads. Then they perform the same token of respect to the pianist who has supported them musically and eased the auditioning ordeal. The end of a ballet audition may be the last bastion of etiquette in the world of teenagers.

By the end of the second round of auditions, Nissinen has chosen six dancers whom he summons to his office for individual closed-door talks. "I told them I liked their dancing but that we didn't have any contracts in the main company now. I asked them what makes them tick, what makes them dance. I want to make the dancers feel good. I also want to get a message out. Everybody who auditions becomes an ambassador. I want them to say that Boston Ballet is respectful, a good place to work.

"At the end of the audition there were some students we invited to the school," Nissinen said. But at the end of a long day, he's hired no one for the company and only one young woman for BB II, Brittany Summer, a 17-year-old about to graduate from the state-funded North Carolina School of the Arts. Another graduate of the North Carolina school, Jaclyn Oakley, was invited to Boston Ballet's trainee program, a notch beneath BB II. Despite the small harvest, it's important to have had the audition. A director doesn't know everyone out there, and Nissinen now has a better feel for the field.

Because Brittany Summer is a North Carolinian, from Gastonia, a small town outside Charlotte, she has had four years of what the ballet world acknowledges as exemplary training, and it has been offered to her at no cost, including room, board, and academic classes. The school, established in 1963, is the envy of parents from other states who have to drive their children to daily dance classes and pay for them. Those aspiring dancers who have to divide their time between academic homework and dance often feel they're shortchanging both. In the North Carolina school, everyone realizes that academic and preprofessional arts classes are equally important. And the dancers in the school get a head start toward their goal of being professionals. They learn repertoire, both classic and modern, that they may later be called on to perform onstage. "We generally have three performances a year," Summer said. "We do *Nutcracker* and two other programs. There's usually one Balanchine piece a year and choreography by some of the teachers. We did *Serenade* in our winter concert. I was also in *La Sonnambula* and *Symphony Concertante*." All three works are by Balanchine.

"When you're a senior, you have conferences with your teachers, and they help you with advice on where to audition." Summer and her mother had flown to New York several times for auditions with companies. Summer didn't get into any of them. "It's nerve-racking," she says. "Company auditions have so many people. You're always nervous about how they make the cuts, and you're always wondering if they'll call out your number. A lot of directors say, 'We'll call you in two weeks.' It was encouraging that Mikko made me an offer right after the audition."

Summer is 5'7½" tall and, of course, taller when she's on pointe. "Mikko told me he had quite a few guys in the company who are over 6' tall," she says with a smile.

Another benefit of acceptance into BB II, aside from a salary, is that the company pays for toe shoes. Even a teenage girl on full scholarship at North Carolina has to buy her own shoes; that generally means her parents end up paying for them, which amounts to hundreds of dollars a year.

An even bigger perk is that Summer and the other female members of BB II got to go on the company's six-week tour to Spain in 2007. (The repertory didn't call for enough male dancers to make it necessary to take along the men of BB II.) "Actually, on the plane ride up to Boston to audition I was talking to my mom about traveling somewhere, maybe to Spain. And then lo and behold, I'm going!"

Summer said her trek to Boston was one of the last auditions she had done. "I was on a different plane every single weekend. I didn't get into other companies, and there weren't any clear answers as to why. Boston was the best I could ask for. There's a certain amount of tension in every audition. You want to do your best in that small window of opportunity." She added, "I was completely not expecting to get into BB II. Other companies I auditioned for were smaller. My parents are really happy about this. Their only desire was that I stay on the East Coast. Boston is a college town, and they were hoping that I would take some college courses."

16

Company Class

What morning prayers are to those in the religious life, company class is to ballet dancers. One wintry day Boston Ballet's dancers straggle into their building's Grand Studio to warm up for their 9:45 class, a more civilized hour than the one when nuns and monks must rouse themselves to perform their rituals. The dancers lug bags as big as carry-on luggage to hold extra shoes, leg warmers, sweatshirts, Band-Aids, and bottled water. The designer water trend has hit the ballet world big-time. Twenty years ago the only water you would see in class came from a watering can, and it was sprinkled on the floor to make the surface less slippery.

Before class, the dancers lie on the floor, stretching their bodies, almost tying them into knots, in preparation for a long day. Their usual schedule is 9:45–6:30, with a 2:30–3:30 lunch break, plus the union-mandated hourly breaks of five minutes (the "fives"). Sometimes the men and women have separate classes because, in terms of bravura steps, they have separate vocabularies to hone, with the women concentrating on pointe work and the men on grand jumps and turns. Sometimes a woman elects to take the men's class. Feijóo does occasionally, not only for a chance to practice a different kind of virtuosity but also, she says, "because I like the teacher."

Ballet master Anthony Randazzo sometimes teaches company class. A member of the Nissinen team that the artistic director has, perhaps unconsciously, been collecting all his life, Randazzo dates from Nissinen's San Francisco era. The two arrived together in 1987 at SFB as soloists and were promoted to principals the next year, and both spent a decade with the company. Like Nissinen, Randazzo had sustained injuries. "My back bothered me the last couple of years of my dancing career. And I sprained my ankle [which can be even more serious than breaking it]. My back pain kept me making little adjustments in my dancing, and I didn't like that." So, while Nissinen went to San Marin, Randazzo returned to his native Detroit area to work with his ballet teacher mother for a year, until Nissinen got on the phone and asked Randazzo to join him in Boston, which he did in August 2002. "When he was setting things up here, Mikko at first wanted to have me teach in the school, then to be a part-time ballet master, then full-time. It's been great. Dancing and teaching and coaching are the only things I ever wanted to do.

"I got to know what direction Mikko was going in, how we could dance as a unified company. Mostly, it's basic and could help any repertory. But there are classes geared toward *Sleeping Beauty* or toward Balanchine. I prepare well for class. I know some teachers enter the studio and just improvise, but I prepare beforehand for the enchaînements," the various combination of steps he'll give the dancers. "I indicate the tempo to the accompanist by snapping my fingers. Mikko is really adamant about controlling the pianist. And no ballet music is played in class. The dancers get enough of that anyway. It would just put them to sleep.

"Teaching men comes naturally to me. But in the women's class they put on pointe shoes, and I feel like I have to prepare six months in advance for that. The ballet masters meet together every day to plan out what's happening, rehearsals and so on. When a guest teacher or choreographer arrives, that immediately throws things out of whack in terms of schedules. We also meet with Mikko every week."

Nissinen says, "We talk about something not working and what to do to make it better." The meetings get very specialized. For instance, after Vives comes to his office to say she's concerned about the way the women's arms are moving in a particular ballet, or that their fingers are curled up instead of stretching to complete the length of the arms, Nissinen will call a meeting concentrated on arms.

Class sometimes focuses on the particular ballet that the dancers are preparing or performing. So Nissinen might work on sections of that choreography, just to make them sharper. He, too, teaches company class, partly as a way to keep tabs on who is doing what correctly and not so well. He adjusts. When the company was rehearsing a couple of particularly difficult and divergent programs, he said, "These two programs are so brutal on the dancers that I try to give them a class that's organic, to get them ready."

The syllabus he uses is from the various styles in which he himself has been trained, taking the best from the best. He views classes as the foundation for improving the company. "Class is not just a warm-up," he adds. "It's a place you come to learn. When I first came, company class was an hour and a quarter. I changed it to an hour and a half, to take advantage of the dancers being very warmed up, so they can practice difficult steps that otherwise might lead to injury."

On this day he is giving class himself to the full company. ("Giving class" is ballet jargon for teaching.) His entrance into the room is matter-of-fact and casual, but it's clear he's in charge, as the dancers peel themselves off the floor and go to the barres that are along the walls and also in the center of the space. Nissinen expects that all dancers, except those who are injured, will attend company class. In such companies as New York City Ballet, there have been some dancers who went to teachers other than Balanchine and his staff. But, of course, New York has a lot more teachers and a lot more pedagogical outlooks on dance than does Boston.

Company class takes place in Boston Ballet's Grand Studio, a pleasant place with high ceilings, floods of natural light, and views of the South End and Back Bay, two of Boston's most picturesque neighborhoods. But the dancers aren't looking at the views. Their eyes are glued to the wall of mirrors, even when it means turning their heads when they should be looking straight ahead. They check and correct their positions relentlessly and sometimes admiringly. In a ballet class each exercise is done first with one leg, then with the other, which usually means a 180 degree turn at the barre, that is, away from the mirror. On one occasion a dancer using a portable barre, in order to keep her eyes on her reflection constantly, goes from one side of the barre to the other as she switches legs. Some choreographers object to this addiction to the mirror, which is a two-dimensional reflection of a three-dimensional art. When visiting Boston to create a new piece for the company in 2006, Mark Morris had the dancers face away from the mirror, so they could feel the movement from the inside rather than merely creating correct shapes.

Between exercises, the dancers fidget, taking off or putting on layers of practice clothing, trying to get themselves to the right temperature so their bodies stay as pliant as possible. Dancers dread feeling a chill. Hence many of them wear down booties for the first part of the class and whenever their feet aren't actually working. The booties are almost comical, turning elegantly arched feet into awkward stumps, like bloated fungi stuck to the bottom of an otherwise slim tree. But they do keep those feet warm.

The rest of their attire is equally eccentric. When a ballet student turns professional, part of the rite of passage is liberation from dress codes. In ballet schools, especially those geared toward training professionals, there is usually a strict dress code. The color of a female student's leotard indicates what level class she's in, while male students generally wear black tights and white T-shirts all the way through school. When they join a company, dancers can wear what they want, and what they want can be bizarre, although Nissinen discourages what he calls "camping gear." One man in the Grand Studio on that winter's day was outfitted as if he were going skiing. Another wore lime green biking shorts. A third sported a lipstick red leotard with gold braid down the sides, part of a recycled costume. A woman who seemed to want to hide herself as much as possible wore an outsized sweatshirt over a tulle skirt. In the area of attire for class, many dancers seem painfully self-conscious while others are peacocks.

They begin with the same exercises they've done virtually every day since age 9 or 10: pliés, the bending of the knees they will use later in the class to propel themselves into the air; tendus, extending the foot to the front, side, or back until it is fully pointed; ronds de jambes, with the working leg circling around the standing one. Company class is a humble return to the beginning. Some teachers, especially those who are also choreographers, which Nissinen is not, use the time to work out individual steps or phrases that will eventually appear onstage. Some obsess over a single step. Nissinen gives several "combinations," as sequences of steps are called, built on tendus. Then there are the Wars of the Ronds de Jambe. Whether the arc that the working leg makes around the standing one should be a small oval shape, or a precise half circle, or more than a half circle is a matter as important to ballet teachers and students as the two-handed vs. the one-handed backhand is to tennis coaches and players.

During class Nissinen walks and talks constantly, stopping only to re-arrange a limb here and there. He's good with metaphor: "You look like you're driving a very big bus," he tells the dancers as a group, meaning that their arms are too far front and too far apart. The dancers get the point, but they smile rather than seeming insulted. Corrections aimed at a single dancer are made with Nissinen speaking up close. There's no yelling from a distance or yelling at all. The stereotype of the nasty teacher belittling dancers once existed at Boston Ballet, with the pre-Nissinen Russian teachers, but by now it's a thing of the past.

At the end of the barre work, which takes roughly half the class, the dancers' legs are soaring in the vicinity of their heads, extending upward in slow, luscious développés or flinging up quickly in grands battements. Professional dancers know their own bodies' needs so well that teachers allow them some leeway. A dancer might sit out an exercise or modify it to accommodate a stress or strain, and teachers will understand that pushing any further would court injury. The dancers, meanwhile, strive to make each exercise beautiful by using the whole body. In an exercise that is mostly about lifting a leg, they will also tilt their heads, turn their shoulders slightly, and curve their arms and fingers to complement that leg.

Leaving the support of the barre—which is supposed to be used minimally to steady the dancers, not as a crutch—the dancers move to the center of the room, where they begin again, with tendus, then continue with lyrical, sustained adagios, then move on to turns and jumps. The teacher demonstrates each exercise, not dancing the steps full out but "marking" them, that is, doing them halfway or using their fingers as stand-ins for what the legs will be doing. The dancers might mark the steps, too, to begin getting the sequence into their muscles, but they might also substitute hands for feet, and so, in a jump calling for crossing the feet in the air, they will practice by crossing their hands.

Class ends with steps that travel on a diagonal across the studio, the longest line in the room. These combinations are the most thrilling, as dancers fly through space with a speed and force that sometimes causes them to screech to a halt before running into the piano in the corner of the room.

Kathleen Breen Combes rehearsing George Balanchine's *Serenade*, choreography by George Balanchine. © The George Balanchine Trust. Photo by Wally Gilbert.

When the class is officially over, the dancers, accustomed to being applauded onstage, applaud their teacher. At the conclusion of the men's class, the teacher says, "Thank you, boys." Adult dancers are still often referred to as "boys" and "girls" until the day they retire. Having been trained in unquestioning obedience, they generally don't object. "They don't mean anything demeaning by it," says Sabi Varga. "If they did, I would object."

After the formal class comes what Nissinen calls "monkey time," when eager dancers with energy to spare practice their tours de force. Varga completes a spectacular series of tours à la seconde, turning on one leg while holding the other one straight out to the side. At the end, sweating but smiling, he explains, "You have to practice them every day. It's like watering a garden."

17

Planning a Season

Programming, choosing dancers, casting ballets and, unfortunately, fund-raising are a contemporary ballet director's biggest tasks. Monica Mason, the artistic director of England's Royal Ballet, said in the spring of 2006 that she was dismayed at having to devote an average of two nights a week to fund-raising because Britain's government is cutting back on support for the arts. Sometimes Nissinen faces two fund-raising events a night.

Programming the ballet seasons is a more interesting challenge, but it, too, is directly affected by financial constraints. Still reeling from the results of the company's *Nutcracker* eviction from the Wang, Nissinen, in early 2006, had to focus on *La Fille mal gardée* and the rest of the something-for-everyone programming for the year. It's a repertory recipe that most U.S. ballet companies now follow. Even at New York City Ballet, the programming is no longer one all-Balanchine evening after another. That model still holds in some eponymous modern dance troupes, such as the Mark Morris Dance Group, where what you see is work by Mark Morris. But none of America's large ballet organizations is driven by a single dance-maker. There has been concern that there aren't classical choreographers around today of sufficient stature to bear that responsibility and that Balanchine, who died in 1983, has no worthy heirs. Even companies with resident choreographers, such as Jorma Elo in Boston, don't bank on them for the bulk of the repertory. So "resident" choreographers wander. At the beginning of 2006, Elo had commissions to make new works for Boston, American Ballet Theatre, New York City Ballet, and the Royal Danish Ballet.

Ballet companies need to attract as wide an audience as possible, from the die-hards who just want to see the nineteenth-century classics endlessly reprised to those who crave premieres. Hence Boston's varied programming in 2006–07, everything from new works by Morris and Elo to the 1841 *Giselle.* Nissinen aims for a balance between the nineteenth-century classics (*Swan Lake, Giselle*), neoclassical works primarily by Balanchine, and twenty-first-century works, to please all factions of the audience. But some people he just can't satisfy. A Cambridge woman—affluent, educated, just the sort of audience member Nissinen wants to cultivate—was delighted to see two all-Balanchine evenings in the 2006–07 season, but incensed that there were only two one-act Balanchine works scheduled for 2007–08. She wrote Nissinen a couple of e-mails stating that because of this, she would not be subscribing to the season. Nissinen responded politely but firmly. "If you are really interested in supporting Balanchine at Boston Ballet, there are opportunities to underwrite a future Balanchine production. This could range from a small ballet with an approximate cost of $50,000 to a full-length ballet in the range of $250,000. To that end, we are interested in doing the charming *Harlequinade* in the future, a piece seldom seen outside of New York City Ballet." (Balanchine's 1965 *Harlequinade,* set to music by Drigo, is in the commedia dell'arte tradition.) Nissinen didn't hear back.

On a bright spring morning in 2006, Nissinen is sitting in his office on the fourth floor of the Boston Ballet building. His office is across the hall from the Grand Studio, so he can drop into rehearsals quickly. On his desk is one of those miniature Japanese gardens with fine sand and a tiny rake. Raking it is the kind of calming, contemplative exercise that you can't imagine Nissinen performing. It's hard even to imagine him sitting still for that long. He's constantly on his feet to talk, teach, or conduct a rehearsal. Nonetheless, when Nissinen came to Boston he bought a nineteenth-century brick row house, renovated it extensively, and installed a Japanese garden in the miniscule backyard. Perhaps that is where he does his contemplation.

Because of the never-ending money problems, the 2006 season wasn't exactly what Nissinen had wanted. He had planned to put Jerome Robbins's 1956 comic classic *The Concert* on the 2006 "Grand Slam" program, along with a work by William Forsythe, the American-born choreographer based in Frankfurt, Germany. Both proved too expensive. For Nissinen, it wasn't just a matter of replacing the two pieces. The replacements had to be of a particular sort. In talking about mixed bills, ballet directors refer to "openers," "middle ballets," and "closers," each of which sets a particular tone that rounds out the evening. "Without *The Concert,* I had to get a closer," Nissinen says. "This turned out to be Val Caniparoli's *Lambarena,* which we could get for less money." The Forsythe replacement turned out to be the first work that Helen Pickett, an American who had danced with Forsythe's company for eleven years, had ever made for a professional company, an opener called *Etesian.*

Extending Nissinen's principle that one dancer's injury is another's opportunity, not being able to afford Forsythe meant Pickett's chance to create her first ballet, which turned out to be a hit. After its opening, Nissinen said, "I've already commissioned another world premiere from her for spring 2008. I've decided I want to promote Helen as well as Jorma."

Keeping exclusive rights to Elo's and Pickett's works is almost as important as promoting them. One problem in American ballet is a certain sameness in the repertories of the big companies. Most of them have works by the usual suspects, including Morris and Balanchine. If Nissinen can give opportunities to less well known young choreographers, he may be able to build the identity that Boston Ballet has lacked.

By the fall of 2007, another $1.5 million had to be shaved off the budget. That meant that Nissinen had to scrap his plan for two Balanchine works—*Monumentum pro Gesualdo* and *Movements for Piano and Orchestra*—that would have accompanied the fall performances of *La Sylphide.* Instead, *La Sylphide* would be accompanied by Balanchine's *Serenade,* which required a smaller orchestra and lower royalties than the two Stravinsky works. The company had danced both works on its 2007 summer tour to Spain, so they were ready to go without many rehearsals.

It was announced in the 2007–08 season release that the year would conclude with the full-length Petipa *La Bayadère.* A few weeks later, another announcement was made. *La Bayadère* was cancelled. It would have cost $800,000 to mount, so it was replaced by Nissinen's own production of *Swan Lake,* which could be put on for $300,000. "It's a freebie for the company. I'll get no royalties," he says, sounding slightly bitter. "Usually when you sell a license to perform a work, you get royalties and a fee, neither of which I'll be paid."

Among Nissinen's goals, even in these lean times, are to add another program to the five the ballet currently offers (not counting *The Nutcracker*), and also to play presenter himself, bringing other troupes to Boston. "It doesn't have to be the biggest of the big," he says, no doubt aware of the large losses that Boston's Celebrity series incurred in bringing England's Royal Ballet and St. Petersburg's Kirov to Boston in recent years.

Nissinen says that he tries to avoid the brand-name ballets that, in theory at least, draw audiences. Most Americans grow up studying literature and music in school. Hardly anyone studies choreography or dance history. For most, it's often the name of the ballet, not its actual choreography, that pulls them into the theater. This can be a recipe for failure, as in Stevenson's *Dracula* and *Cleopatra,* both performed before Nissinen's arrival. Both were artistic disasters, drowned in décor that obscured what little actual choreography there was.

Not all story ballets are duds, of course. Ashton's *La Fille mal gardée,* which opened the 2006 season, also tells a story, but it is a masterpiece. Boston had performed the work in 2003. One reason for the encore was that Boston had licensed it for five years, and time was running out. The company generally tries for a five- to seven-year license to amortize the initial cost of acquiring a ballet. With seven years, a troupe can conceivably repeat a hit in several seasons without an additional fee. On the other hand, if a new work proves to be a mistake, a company may try to sell the production as soon as possible to another, hoping that the other company hasn't read the reviews.

Maina Gielgud returned to Boston in 2007 to coach her version of *Giselle.* Lest anyone miss the point, the program read, "Maina Gielgud's Production of *Giselle,* Staged and Rehearsed by Maina Gielgud." She talked about what she thinks are the biggest problems facing the field in the early twenty-first century, not a high point in the art form. She mentioned the lack of adequate rehearsal time as one factor dragging ballet down. "That lack makes ballet ever less popular all over the world," she said. "Dancers' techniques are ever better. Their legs soar up to their ears, and their pirouettes seem endless. But there's not much attention paid to the subtleties of the upper body, the expression of the head, arms, and hands, which are necessary even in abstract ballets."

Nissinen's version of this lament is that "the passion has gone out of ballet" over the course of his career. "For the last forty years ballet has gotten better and better technically. But the chisel is not the work of art. It's just a tool to make art. In America there used to be a flame, a passion about ballet. Then everything became institutionalized and corporate. It lacked soul."

Gielgud also mourns, as she says, "the disappearance of stars, the growing fashion in almost all classically based companies of not having stars. It's very odd that, in this age when athletes and movie actors are increasingly promoted as stars, ballet dancers aren't. There's a flaw in the logic there. There used to be all this promotion around Margot Fonteyn, Rudolf Nureyev, and Mikhail Baryshnikov. When they stopped dancing, attendance at the ballet dropped."

Nissinen's biggest accomplishment of the 2006–07 season was the summer tour to Spain. The tour came about because the ex-husband of Ada Casanovas, the tour presenter, was a Cuban dancer. He knew that Lorna Feijóo was in Boston and suggested that Casanovas call her. After the initial contact with Feijóo, Casanovas got in touch with Nissinen and flew to Boston to see the company perform, and the deal was done. It was a break-even proposition financially, Nissinen said, with the festivals paying all the company's expenses.

Nissinen had been itching for the company to get out of Boston, to visit places that might appreciate his dancers more than the home crowd did. The last time the company had had a foreign tour was 1991. "I don't mind tough times," Nissinen said, "but there has to be some sun mixed in there, too." The company would get plenty of that in Spain.

18

The Spring 2006 Season

The spring 2006 season opened with *Fille.* Then came a program called "Grand Slam," featuring contemporary works by Jorma Elo, the San Francisco–based Val Caniparoli, Mark Morris, the most sought-after choreographer on the planet, and Helen Pickett, something of a dark horse, whose work is based on improvisation. "An Evening of Russian Ballet," largely made up of excerpts from the classics, followed. The spring season finished in May with the premiere of Elo's *Carmen* paired with Balanchine's *Serenade.*

The company disbanded for most of the summer and, after reuniting in August, prepared to perform Rudolf Nureyev's *Don Quixote* in October, then wind up the calendar year with the holiday run of *The Nutcracker,* thirty-eight performances of it, all of which Nissinen dutifully attended.

The dancers barely had time to catch their breath before launching into the spring 2007 season, which opened with George Balanchine's *A Midsummer Night's Dream.* Then came a program called "New Visions," with a premiere by Elo, Christopher Wheeldon's *Polyphonia,* and *Sonata for Two Pianos and Percussion* by Val Caniparoli. A "Classic Balanchine" program with the master's *Ballo della Regina, La Valse,* and *The Four Temperaments* followed, and the season concluded with Gielgud's *Giselle.*

La Fille mal gardée, March 9–12, 2006

Rehearsal

"Let's start with the entrance of the chickens," says Alexander Grant, as a flock of young women who have spent at least ten years of hard training to be swans or maybe the Firebird but definitely not chickens assemble for their entrance in the Grand Studio at the top of Boston Ballet's home. Elbows and knees pumping, they make their entrance in *Fille* as baby fowl.

Grant was in Boston to stage *Fille* for the company, as he had three years earlier. Viewed by many as the greatest of all British character dancers—and that's a major statement in the country of Shakespeare, where acting in the ballet is considered as important as bravura technique—Grant, at age 81, can instantly assume any role in the ballet, from the teenaged heroine Lise to her crotchety, ambitious mother, the Widow Simone. The British choreographer Frederick Ashton created the role of the doltish Alain for Grant, who danced it at *Fille's* 1960 premiere. Grant knows the posture and gestures of every role, and in assuming them for the Boston dancers he can convey them instantly, as no videotape or film or a coach who learned the work thirdhand ever could. Grant is the living link to *Fille.* Photographs of him in Alain's signature gesture, jumping with a red umbrella between his legs, as if riding a toy horse, attest to his gifts as a character dancer, a category more respected in Europe than in America, where athleticism is prized above all other qualities. "I danced Alain all over the world," he says. "It became my favorite part."

Fille's plot is simplicity itself. The Widow Simone is force-feeding Lise the idea of Alain as a husband because his father is rich. Lise, meanwhile, prefers the handsome but impoverished farmer Colas. The story ends as you knew it would the moment the curtain went up, with Lise marrying Colas. So it's what happens en route that counts.

As the scenario suggests, *La Fille mal gardée* is a comedy, the rarest form of classical dance, which lends itself more easily to tragic endings. The role of the Widow is always played by a man dressed en travestie. Christopher Budzynski is one of Boston's Widows this time out. For rehearsal, where an approximation of the onstage costume is all that is necessary, he wears what appears to be a largish dishtowel wrapped around his head and a circle skirt that Annette Funicello might have sported in the 1950s. If you saw him outside the building on a sidewalk, you would cross the street.

In one rehearsal a few days before the March 9 opening of *Fille,* Grant coaches Budzynski on derriere-wiggling, which, in *Fille,* is an expression of Widow Simone's chagrin at Lise's intractability. Budzynski complies gamely.

Jared Redick, as the idiot Alain, spends much of the rehearsal mastering the not inconsiderable feat of dancing with that red umbrella tucked between his legs. "When I was a teenager dancing with San Francisco Ballet, the company did *Fille,* and what I thought about Alain was, 'What a stupid role.' But I was young." Now in his mid-thirties, he's changed his mind. After the run of the show, he said, "I thought it was a blast, the most fun I've ever had in a ballet. And having Alexander Grant to coach me, the man who was the original Alain, was an incomparable privilege."

Fille is commonly called "the oldest extant ballet in the repertory." But *oldest* is a term that bears some explaining when used in conjunction with choreography. Classical ballet as we know it evolved from sixteenth-century court dance, performed by the courtiers themselves. As the choreography became ever more complex, the aristocrats became the audience, and professional ballet was born.

Fille dates from 1789, or at least its plot does. Jean Dauberval scripted the scenario and also created the choreography. Versions of the ballet have been regularly performed by companies in Paris, London, St. Petersburg, and elsewhere ever since.

But the 1789 *Fille* would have looked vastly different from the productions seen today. The ballet wouldn't have been performed on pointe, for instance. Toe shoes were an early nineteenth-century invention meant literally to put women on pedestals, to make them seem to float like sylphs and other unworldly creatures. Nowadays, *Fille* is performed on pointe not because Lise and the other farm girls are supernatural creatures but because audiences expect virtuosity. The same goes for other bravura elements. No eighteenth-century ballerina could lift her foot up past her ear, but that kind of height, called "extension," is now what audiences want to see and what dancers want to show them.

Video cameras weren't around in 1789, so we will never really know what *Fille*'s original choreography was. This is the norm in the ballet world. We won't ever really know the entire original choreography of the Tchaikovsky/Petipa ballets, either, although extensive written notes, dancers' memoirs, photographs, and, most of all, the Tchaikovsky scores provide clues of the kind that don't exist with *Fille*, which was first set to popular French tunes padded by an unidentified composer. The score has been tinkered with ever since. Jonathan McPhee says the *Fille* score Ashton used was based on an 1828 version by French operatic composer Louis Joseph Ferdinand Hérold, elegantly enhanced by Ashton's colleague John Lanchbery, then the principal conductor of the Royal Ballet. The result, the score Boston uses, includes everything from a traditional Lancashire clog dance to snippets of Donizetti and Rossini. Lanchbery, says McPhee, was "very good at taking bits from various classical works and 'whipping them up' in a British pantomime way that was quite effective theatrically."

However, a whipped-up collage can't give many clues to the original choreography. Sometimes a prop can help. *Fille* has several signature props: Alain's umbrella, the butter churn, and pink silk ribbons are among the most notable, and they're so integral to the story that it's likely they were there all along. Early twentieth-century photographs show Anna Pavlova wielding those ribbons. They're multipurpose. They serve as reins to drive a cart. In one pas de deux Colas and Lise make a cat's cradle out of them. Most dramatically, they act as Lise's partner in one scene when, standing on the toes of one foot, the other foot in the air in the bent-knee position called attitude, she clutches ribbons that fan out from her hand like the spokes of an umbrella, each held at the other end by one of the eight dancers who play her friends. It's the tension of the ribbons that keeps Lise from falling over as she turns on pointe, but it reads as the sheer force of friendship holding her up.

Kuranaga sums up *Fille*'s ribbon challenge. "You can never control them. It's not like your body. I had one show when the ribbons went wrong. I think that anyone in the audience who really knew the choreography would have known something was wrong. My ribbon was supposed to be wrapped around my waist, but it was around my chest. If it had moved up any more, it could have gotten stuck around my neck." A strangled Lise.

Misa Kuranaga rehearsing *La Fille mal gardée*. Photos by Wally Gilbert.

Alexander Grant coaching Misa Kuranaga for *La Fille mal gardée*. Photo by Wally Gilbert.

Ashton, says Grant, never wanted to choreograph *Fille* in the first place. He had been busy creating ballets for the principal muse of his career, Margot Fonteyn, who was definitely not the bouncy comedienne that is Lise. But Tamara Karsavina, a legendary star of Diaghilev's Ballets Russes, was constantly prodding Ashton to remake *Fille*. Dorothy Wordsworth's writings and John Constable's paintings had made him yearn to create a similarly unspoiled, idyllic countryside onstage, but it was Karsavina performing the mime scene in *Fille*, in which the heroine imagines herself married to her hero and the mother of three children, that persuaded the choreographer to take on the challenge.

Grant recalled that once Ashton signed on to re-create *Fille*, the steps poured out of him as smoothly as the butter Lise churns in one of the ballet's most charming scenes. The choreographer, says Grant, never devised a step before entering the studio where the dancers awaited him. In the case of *Fille*, Grant says, "He would make a variation [a solo dance] in one rehearsal and hardly change any of it afterward." *Fille* was also "the only ballet he ever made that was unanimously acclaimed by the critics on opening night."

This was a particular triumph because Ashton's *Fille* premiered in 1960, when what Grant calls "kitchen sink" ballets were dominant. By "kitchen sink" he means Beat Age fare, with grim everyday subjects. *Fille*, at least on the surface, is all froth. But Grant points out that the original ballet was created at the time of the French Revolution, which may account for the themes of defiance and equality in the plot. Lise is a rebel, and the humble, hard-working Colas comes across as a finer fellow than either Alain or his overbearing father, who belong to the affluent landowning class.

While superficially *Fille* is merely fun, it never stoops to slapstick. Part of what keeps *Fille* from being merely a jolly good evening in the theater is the many influences at work on Ashton at the time he made it. They give the choreography complexity and depth. Ashton had gone to Denmark in 1955 to make a *Romeo and Juliet* for the Royal Danish Ballet, a company indelibly associated with the nineteenth-century story ballets of August Bournonville. The Danes are great mimes, as Ashton also was. (Grant recalls Ashton being frequently summoned to entertain England's late Queen Mother with his impersonations, including one of her predecessors, Queen Victoria.)

Nelson Madrigal
rehearsing *La Fille
mal gardée* for
Mikko Nissinen.
Photo by Wally
Gilbert.

There is a particular sweetness to Bournonville's dances, and "there's some of that charm in *Fille*," Grant says. He also recalls that the Bolshoi's visit to London in the 1950s came as a revelation to the genteel English ballet world. The Moscow company's Soviet-era pyrotechnics made their mark even on Ashton, whose natural sensibility was far more subtle and who never used gymnastics for their own sake. "There are some pretty hefty lifts in *Fille*," Grant notes, "but they're woven into the fabric of the dance."

At his death in 1988, Ashton left the rights to *Fille* to Grant. It is common practice for choreographers to bequeath their works to dancers who were in the studio when the ballets were created, who performed in the original, and who can be relied on to safeguard their integrity.

Grant now teaches *Fille* all over the world, and it is up to him to decide which ballet companies can perform the Ashton masterpiece. Whether the company requesting the work is in Turkey or Tbilisi, the system is the same. Grant, or his delegate, visits the troupe to make sure that the dancers are technically and stylistically capable of executing the deceptively simple looking choreography. Then Grant or an assistant shows up for a few weeks of intensive rehearsing and coaching, to make sure they've got it right. "I've had to say no a few times," he says of the dozens of companies that have asked for the rights to the perennially popular ballet.

Performance

Despite the keenly felt absence of the injured Larissa Ponomarenko, *Fille* is once again a success for Boston, both artistically and at the box office. Part of its wistful allure in our age is that its characters make their own entertainment, through clog dancing or bouncing around to a tambourine, snapping their fingers and clapping. They don't have TVs, CDs, or DVDs to stare at until comatose. Through their bodies, and at the end through their voices, when they all exit singing "la, la, la," they connect to each other in a more visceral way than we do today. For a couple of hours at least, *Fille* makes it seem that their life is enviable compared with life in the twenty-first century.

It was certainly the triumph of the spring season for Kuranaga. She and Grant got along wonderfully, and he encouraged her to develop the most refined quality in Ashton choreography: épaulement, the movement of the back that flows through the shoulders and arms, giving them a liquid quality and liveliness. In America, épaulement is often sacrificed. Jumping ever higher and performing ever more pirouettes, athleticism again is the goal. Kuranaga is a great athlete. But she understands how not to emphasize that onstage.

"Grand Slam," March 16–26, 2006

"Grand Slam" included works by Mark Morris, Jorma Elo, Val Caniparoli, and Helen Pickett. The title traded on Boston's love of baseball, epitomized by the Red Sox, with the company hoping for home runs with four works. Morris is the most famous contemporary choreographer in the world. Elo was at the time still better known in Europe than in the United States. Pickett was making her first work ever for a company of any significance, while Caniparoli was a veteran who had spent most of his career with San Francisco Ballet and is known primarily for works that are instantly likeable and related to pop culture.

Etesian

Pickett's piece is titled *Etesian,* the name of a fresh northeasterly wind from the Mediterranean that blows over the Aegean. "I took that name because I love how sound is carried on wind," she says. "You turn to see where it's coming from, and you can't. It's a conduit for the ethereal, a conduit for information that you can't really point at. You can't grab it, but the strength is there. That's dance, too, just the moment onstage. You can't capture it."

Etesian opens with sixty seconds of one of the most daring Boston Ballet dancers, Kathleen Breen Combes, improvising on her own. An anxiety-producing task, it was also mesmerizing, a fine start for a fine ballet that ends in stillness.

One of the scariest things a choreographer can ask a ballet-trained dancer to do is to improvise. From the age of 10 or so, ballet dancers are taught to obey orders and to be precise. After ten or twelve years of this regime they feel like freezing in place if asked to be spontaneous—which some of them had to be in *Etesian.* "With the piece I used several improvisation modalities," Pickett explains. "In Frankfurt, we were all ballet-trained and did a barre every day. This work is based in that." Half the dancers in *Etesian* improvise. Those who don't engage in "reading," which means that one dancer takes off from another. Ideally, the audience ends up able to pick up on that.

Etesian is set to a comfortingly familiar blend of excerpts of Bach and Beethoven. The most innovative choreographers often gravitate toward the most traditional music: it's hard to say whether they intend it to bolster their work or they just love it. Pickett is in the "I just love it" camp. "Mikko said to me, 'You know, you're using some of the world's greatest music in this piece.' I said, 'I know. But it's close to my heart. It's sublime.'"

Ballet has a specific vocabulary. And so does Pickett, even beyond William Forsythe's. "Foot description" is one of her terms. "It investigates all sides of the feet," she says, an idea that strikes terror in the hearts of ballet dancers who have learned to point their feet perfectly. "Using all sides of the feet is scary because the 'sickle' factor comes in." Sickling is bending the foot so that the weight is opposite the instep, a potential source of major injuries for dancers if they put weight on that improperly positioned foot. If they don't, it's just a different shape. "It creates completely new positions that I find beautiful," Pickett says. "It can be just a punctuation, a comma or semicolon."

"Manipulation" is another of Pickett's terms, wherein "you actively move your own body, taking your hand to move your head, for instance." "Piecing out the body" is yet another of her elements. She defines it as taking one body part at a time to create a conventional ballet position that a dancer would otherwise achieve all together, in an instant.

To reassure the Boston dancers about her version of improv, she showed a video of some of her New York work. "I'm on a mission to reeducate people on improvisation," she says. "The Boston Ballet dancers had fear, because improv is what they've forever been told not to do. That ever so beautiful anxiety paralyzes you. You get over it through practice. That's why I say nice things to my dancers all the time. I have to build trust in the room. I always remind them of their courage. 'You did a courageous step,' I'll say to them. I do a lot of work initially with eyes closed, because the toughest judge is you yourself. Improv is not as foreign as everybody thinks. *Etesian* is my first real piece, and man, did I learn a lot. The Boston Ballet is a diplomatic, generous place. It makes you want to act well. How can you act badly when you're in this nurturing generosity?"

Plan to B

Jorma Elo's *Plan to B* was the first and arguably the finest of the works Boston Ballet's resident choreographer has made for the company. Premiered in 2004, it was reprised in 2006. Its score, by the great seventeenth-century German composer Heinrich Ignaz von Biber, is a gently shivering violin piece, and the six dancers match that dynamic.

The choreography is filled with great virtuosity—pirouettes, leaps, turns in the air—but this is a virtuosity that doesn't sell itself. Elo plays it down. The piece goes nonstop, with none of the usual preparations that clue you that a particularly difficult step is coming up.

While there are solos in this dense twelve-minute piece, the emphasis is on dancers playing off each other, in pairs or in larger groups. They spin each other around or send each other soaring in the air. There's a great moment when a man causes a standing woman's body to ripple head to toe. The most unpredictable part of the piece is its ending. It just stops, with one woman hunched over, four men behind her, and the other woman missing in action.

Up and Down

The latest of Mark Morris's works created for Boston was the 2006 *Up and Down,* set to Alexander Glazunov's Quartet for Four Saxophones in B Major, op. 109.

The title reflects the work. Morris is never less than a superb craftsman, ever responsive to his score, but this is not one of his finest pieces. Nonetheless, there are some delightful moments. My favorite is when Lorna Feijóo makes her way through a crowd, paying them no attention whatsoever, walking nonchalantly and flat-footed into the wings. She's got the feminine authority of the character Lucy in the *Peanuts* comics.

Lambarena

"I just signed my thirty-third dancer contract with San Francisco Ballet," Val Caniparoli said in 2006. "I'm a principal character dancer. I want a gold walker. Mostly now, I perform in story ballets, like the father in *Prodigal Son,* the Widow Simone in *La Fille mal gardée,* Madge, the witch in *La Sylphide,* and the evil magician Von Rothbart in *Swan Lake.* Helgi Tomasson was the first director in this country to have a category called 'character dancer.' In other American companies it has tended to be the kids in the corps who are stuck with these roles, so of course they lack maturity and training in acting, which are essential if you're going to play a 60- or 70-year-old demon."

Caniparoli's contribution to "Grand Slam" is an exemplary "closer" ballet, *Lambarena,* which premiered in 1995 and is now done by more than fifteen companies. It fuses African music with passages by Bach, whose music always seems infinitely flexible. Caniparoli enlisted advice from African dance experts on how to get the dancers to loosen up their hips, which ballet dancers are trained to keep still, and how to undulate their shoulders and curve their backs as if they had been born in Senegal. Nonetheless, the sight of ballet dancers shaking their slim hips like African fertility figures remains a bit strange.

Compared with the other three works on "Grand Slam," *Lambarena* is easy watching and listening. "It's gotten mixed reviews, but audiences seem to like it," its creator says. Is it his signature work? "I hope I haven't done my signature ballet yet." Now in his mid-fifties, he's conscious that "I'll never be one of the anointed ones, but I work as much as Mark Morris and Christopher Wheeldon," both touted as choreographers to watch from the get-go. "And I'm on the same programs with them."

"An Evening of Russian Ballet," May 4–7, 2006

Among other things, this program proved that there is no clear-cut entity that is "Russian Ballet." In many people's minds the phrase is synonymous with the late nineteenth-century ballets of Marius Petipa, who was responsible for *The Sleeping Beauty* and much of *Swan Lake.* (By the way, Petipa was French, not Russian. His birthplace was Marseilles.) For others, Russian Ballet means Diaghilev's Ballets Russes, and for other balletomanes the definition stretches to include the Soviet bravura style that wowed New York in the 1950s.

Boston's Russian program was a bits-and-pieces affair bracketed by act 3 of *Raymonda* and *Les Noces* and filled out with music by Tchaikovsky and Mussorgsky, without dancing, which added to the ambience but made you wonder why, with all the fine dancers and fledgling choreographers in Boston, there wasn't choreography to accompany the

music. While Petipa's *Raymonda* is not in the same league as his *Sleeping Beauty* and *Swan Lake,* the two greatest masterpieces of nineteenth-century classicism, it has lovely passages. The third act is, like the last act of *Sleeping Beauty,* a wedding scene, all pomp and processional. Unlike *Sleeping Beauty,* though, with its strong metaphorical content in the first acts, *Raymonda's* plot is lame, so excerpting act 3 is an audience-friendly move. In keeping with the nineteenth-century tradition of national dances in ballets—think of the Chinese, Arabian, and other variations in *Nutcracker*—the last act of *Raymonda* has a Hungarian flavor. *Flavor* is the right term in describing these national dances, which are essentially classical but accessorized with gestures the audience will recognize as Chinese, Spanish, or whatever. In *Raymonda* the eponymous heroine, as usual in Petipa ballets, has the most interesting choreography, especially in her final variation, where she launches into a series of passés. As her standing leg rises on pointe, her working leg rises so its foot is at the standing leg's knee. The result is a triangle. The excitement in *Raymonda's* passés comes from changes in tempo and mood. They start

Tutus for *Raymonda,* act 3. Photo by Wally Gilbert

Kathleen Breen Combes and Sabi Varga rehearsing *Spring Waters*. Photo by Wally Gilbert.

out languid and teasing, as if she were calling attention to her beauty and her position in the world. Gradually they accelerate to lightning fast, as if she were calling attention to her power. She is having one great time performing this step, and she takes the audience right along.

Between *Raymonda* and *Les Noces* came a series of short works including *The Dying Swan* and the virtuoso duet *Spring Waters* by the Soviet-era choreographer Asaf Messerer, whose style is as close as ballet comes to acrobatics. The most thrilling moment in the duet is when the ballerina is hoisted, with seeming effortlessness, onto the upstretched arm of her partner. She sits on his hand, ideally without wobbling, but instead looking secure and triumphant. (In a rehearsal with Viktor Plotnikov coaching Kathleen Breen Combes and Sabi Varga, Plotnikov told Combes, "You can't adjust once you're up there, and you can't look down once you're up because it's too scary.") In this particular lift, once the woman is "up there," her partner looks like a waiter holding a tray high above his head as he tries to navigate his way through a crowded restaurant. *Spring Waters* is a sure-fire hit with the general ballet audience, but not necessarily a favorite with connoisseurs. ("Do I think that *Spring Waters* is a masterpiece?" Nissinen asked rhetorically during a rehearsal. "Of course not. But it certainly is entertaining. The one masterpiece on this program is *Les Noces*.")

Choreographed in 1923 by Bronislava Nijinska, sister of Vaslav Nijinsky, and set to one of Stravinsky's most somber and severe scores, *Les Noces* is ostensibly about a peasant wedding in Holy Mother Russia at some point in the country's distant past, but it also alludes to the twentieth-century uprising of the proletariat in that country. The ritual unfolds in four scenes: "The Blessing of the Bride," "The Blessing of the Bridegroom," "The Bride's Departure from Her Parents' House," and "The Wedding Feast." The choreography asks ballet dancers to use their training, but also to go against it, in deliberately awkward turned-in positions, with clenched fists and hunched-over torsos. Where usually they are as light as possible, here they stomp their feet into the floor, as if subduing the earth beneath them. Where usually they are as pliant as possible, here they are stiff, almost as if partially paralyzed. Precision and perfect unisons are utterly necessary to pull off *Les Noces* because of the sheer starkness of the choreography. The effort is worth it: this ballet, more than eighty years old, seems more modern than much of today's modern dance.

Serenade and *Carmen,* May 11–21, 2006

Serenade

Jorma Elo's third world premiere created for Boston Ballet, *Carmen,* was paired with my desert island ballet, the 1934 *Serenade.* The first work that Balanchine made in America, this most Euclidean of ballets, filled with one breathtaking pattern after another, is probably the most photogenic classical ballet in history and a landmark in the abstract choreography that Balanchine went on to pioneer. Set to Tchaikovsky's Serenade in C for String Orchestra, op. 46, it is especially memorable for the lovely formations the corps settles into after rushing around the stage. After one Boston Ballet rehearsal of *Serenade,* Trinidad Vives noted that there is an element of improvisation in the piece, as the dancers run from one pattern to the next. The reason, Vives said, is like traffic control, so the dancers don't run into each other but instead get into the right position at the right time. (Because the sizes of stages differ, a ballet that involves so much running around has to be carefully rehearsed to suit the scale of each new venue.)

Serenade opens with a group of women lifting one arm and flexing their wrists, as if they are saluting the sun. Then, in a unison that can make audiences gasp, they turn out their legs and feet in a quick, unexpected gesture, assuming the basic stance of classical ballet, as if this were the dawn of the art. The turned-out position empowers classical dancers, enabling them to show those highly trained legs to full advantage.

Thus energized, the dancers engage in a feast of inventive patterns that prove Balanchine the heir to the "white" acts of *Giselle* and *Swan Lake,* where the corps create long diagonal lines, circles, and other geometric shapes. Balanchine took that concept and made it ever more complex, more kaleidoscopic. In *Serenade* a quartet of women with arms lifted in circles above their heads look like a fan opening. A line of women sink slowly to the floor by doing splits, without giving that movement its usual acrobatic quality. This sisterhood then cross their arms and hold hands: physical linking of a corps of women became a favorite Balanchine motif, a way to extend a gesture to fill the stage. It happens repeatedly in *Concerto Barocco* and *Theme and Variations.* Another motif in *Serenade* that Balanchine would reuse is having one dancer put his or her hand over another's eyes, temporarily robbing the other dancer of sight, making that dancer dependent. In one of *Serenade's* most magical moments, a woman assumes an arabesque on pointe while a man, partly hidden by her tulle gown, holds her leg and rotates her. She is at once both still and in motion.

Most of the steps in *Serenade* aren't difficult individually. Balanchine created the work for students from his recently opened School of American Ballet, and although they were trained, early photographs of the piece indicate that their technique was limited. In addition to being hauntingly beautiful, *Serenade* is a teaching ballet, to show dancers how to operate as a unit onstage.

This is the most abstract of ballets, plotless, although viewers are always tempted to read a story into the choreography and even nickname the dancers: the Dark Angel, the Russian Girl, the Jumping Girl. There are many more women than men in the piece, reflecting the percentages of Americans dancing classical ballet in the 1930s (and today). In the sublime ending, one ballerina is gently lifted into the air and borne offstage in a deep backbend, as if being carried into the moonlight, with an entourage of woman doing bourrées behind her. It's as if she has completed her mission—Kirstein's mission—of introducing classical ballet to America.

Carmen

Serenade preceded Elo's *Carmen,* as if the Balanchine were a soothing balm before the inevitable storm of the Spanish love tragedy, based on Prospero Merimee's novella and set to Rodion Shchedrin's adaptation of Bizet's score that makes the music more danceable. *Carmen* was Jorma Elo's first story ballet. Setting the tale of betrayal and death in the tough, contemporary, even violent world of today, Elo turned the women into supermodels and the men into sinisterly sleek businessmen. The opening night reviews were resoundingly negative. I saw the work three times and thought that after the third I had finally understood what Elo was trying to accomplish, which was a fresh reading of a score and story that had descended into the realm of cliché. Having faith in his childhood friend, and not wanting to dump the production, with its new sets and costumes, immediately after its premiere, Nissinen said that he was programming a revival, with a makeover involving an eight-minute cut in the work, for a season coming soon.

Jorma Elo rehearsing a dancer for *Carmen*. Photo by Wally Gilbert.

The women in *Carmen* slither down a platform that reads as a runway on which the models are ogled by the men. At one point the women shed their flirty little skirts to wear what appear to be tight-fitting, shiny bathing suits.

There's a certain freshness in Elo's *Carmen*, the biggest work, with twenty-eight dancers, he's attempted to date, and the only one with a story and gestures that refer to aspects of it, including a moment when Carmen raises her hands beside her head, emulating a bull's horns.

Among the sites of the original is a tobacco factory where the women work. If Elo's characters are smoking, it's not tobacco. However much plasticity Elo pours into the writhing and seductive movement, it remains unsentimental. It's also crowded. There are so many little solos and duets crammed into the piece that sometimes it is hard to figure out where the principals have gone. The dancers never really do disappear for long. They're often in the wings, entirely visible to the audience.

The Boston dancers, more familiar than any other company with Elo's work, took the opportunity to become characters instead of ab-

stractions, although Elo's nonstop, fidgety movement never settles down enough for the real passion the story calls for. Elo's Don José came across like the military dictator of a corrupt little country. Mercedes's hands claw at Don José, in an attempt to hang onto him. Elo has become celebrated for using the entire body: not for him ballet's usual static hips and gently curved arms. His choreography calls for swiveling hips and fingers that act like weapons.

Elo is, at bottom, a cerebral choreographer whose intellect is ill suited to a tale of passion and revenge. Nonetheless, *Carmen* is worth more than one viewing because of its movement invention, even if that variety of movement isn't a natural match for the story. Elo is like that. He deconstructs music, choreography, and here a classic plot. As I was leaving the Wang after one *Carmen,* a woman said to her companion, "I wanted something more Spanish." I longed to say to her, "You can get that elsewhere."

Roman Rykine and Carlos Molina in *Carmen* at the Citi Performing Arts Center Wang Theatre. Photo by Wally Gilbert.

19

The Fall 2006 Season

Don Quixote, October 19–29, 2006

Rudolf Nureyev's version of the robust comic ballet based on Cervantes's novel has proven to be one of Boston Ballet's most popular works. Nureyev came to Boston himself to teach the work. A demanding, even insulting coach, he terrified the dancers with his barbs. But he got results.

At times the production has been insufficiently rehearsed, and that showed onstage. Without Nureyev to put fire and fear into the dancers, they sometimes took it easy. However, Boston Ballet's 2006 revival of the work was rigorously coached and brought back to its full strength.

Nureyev had firm views about the atmosphere of the work. The climax of the ballet is a wedding pas de deux for Kitri and Basilio. This duet is often performed out of context, excerpted for galas and other special occasions, where it becomes a party piece, full of bravura steps. In his staging of the complete work, Nureyev wanted the duet to be solemn, like a real marriage ceremony.

Don Quixote also marked Larissa Ponomarenko's return to the stage after taking most of the year off to let her foot heal. "It was so hard for me to start up again," she says. "I had to wear that boot [a walking cast] for so many months. It was my left foot, and everything for the ballerina in *Don Q* is on the left foot, including the thirty-two fouetté turns. There were days in the studio when I would start crying."

The Nutcracker, November 24–December 30, 2006.

As much as audiences love the Christmas classic, the dancers find a month's worth of it tedious. It's not unheard of for a dancer to play as many as twelve roles in *The Nutcracker* over its run, none of them particularly memorable.

When the ballet premiered at the Maryinsky in St. Petersburg on December 18, 1892, no one predicted the icon (and moneymaker) it would become. Indeed, the ballet was at first panned in Russia. (See Jennifer Fisher's 2003 book *"Nutcracker" Nation.*)

Balanchine himself played a mouse in the Maryinsky production. In the United States, it was his 1954 staging of the holiday confection for New York City Ballet that got things rolling. But initially, Balanchine's version was also panned, at least by John Martin, the powerful dance critic of the *New York Times.* His commentary prefigured the ambiguous role that *Nutcracker* would play later on in many U.S. companies, including Boston's. "The greatest peril [was] its box office success," he wrote in a February 3, 1954, review. "The indisputable fact is that [it] is an inferior ballet. It denies the very basis of 'the Balanchine revolution,' which has changed the very art of the ballet by showing it to be an art of dancing—not of miming, spectacle, or story-telling. There is very little dancing in *The Nutcracker.* To make matters no better, it is played largely by children. That it drew a new audience is undeniable, but once it got them there it showed them absolutely nothing to win them to the ballet. It is an outworn superstition that by giving people what is inferior you will ultimately win them to what is superior. The sad and terrible result is usually that they become so much more deeply attached to the inferior that it becomes financially impossible to give them anything else."

As Martin prophesized, American ballet companies became dependent on *Nutcracker* box office business to a dangerous degree; hence Boston Ballet's panic when their production was bumped from the Wang. In that huge house the company had milked the ballet for all it could, selling CDs, mini-tutus, and other paraphernalia, and also offering hotel packages including limousine service to the ballet.

Many if not most artistic directors and choreographers put their personal stamp on their company's *Nutcracker.* Some versions, for instance, stress the protagonist's budding sexuality, with Clara (or Marie, her alias) an adolescent on the brink of indoctrination to the grown-up world. But Boston Ballet founder E. Virginia Williams, not one for kinky plot twists, wanted a production with a "G" rating, a *Nutcracker* for children. (There's a limit, however. Every year Boston has to remind audiences that 5 is the suggested minimum age, and all children must have their own tickets. There are, however, booster seats for rent so that the shortest fans have a chance of seeing what's going on.)

In the past, Boston Ballet programs credited several individuals with the *Nutcracker* choreography. The result, naturally, was to exacerbate the lack of continuity inherent in the ballet. It's a bunch of diverse dances strung together. The leading couple, the Sugar Plum Fairy and her Cavalier, have a single pas de deux at the end. We never learn anything about them except that they seem to rule a kingdom devoted to candy.

In Boston Ballet's production, the scale of both dancing and décor was made to fit the Wang, so both at the Colonial and then at the Opera House some elements are missing and others look condensed. At the Wang, Clara and Drosselmeier, the elderly eccentric who sets the plot in motion, were always observers at the edge of the stage in the second act, so they could see the various dances being performed for their pleasure. In the Opera House, Nissinen had to relocate them to upstage center, where they sit sharing a throne and looking as if they're on a crowded bus. They're not only a distraction to the audience, but they can see only the backs of the dancers meant to welcome them to the Palace of Sweets.

Boston's various versions have relied heavily on the elaborate sets by Helen Pond and Herbert Senn, so the national variations—Spanish, Arabian, Chinese, and Russian—each had their own theater within a theater, with signature attributes reinforcing the dancers' identity, all within the larger proscenium. This part of the set, alas, is too big to fit into the Opera House. There remains, however, a particularly majestic play of scale so that the Mouse King (the villain in act 1, whom Clara attacks with her shoe) enters on a sofa big enough for King Kong. Oh, and there is Flying by Foy as well. Clara and Drosselmeier leave the "real" world at the end of act 1 in a hot air balloon. At the ballet's end, they return to reality by the same means.

Nissinen's *Nutcracker* is streamlined, with real dancing from the start, as opposed to some productions that open with long scenes of tedious mime. He skips some of the cornier gestures of his predecessors. The

Polichinelles, small children who emerge from under Mother Ginger's skirt, don't do the tacky fanny-bumping bit of previous productions. Nissinen has, though, wisely kept a couple of more appropriate touches added by his predecessors. One is the choreography by Daniel Pelzig, an earlier company choreographer, of the battle between the mice and the toy soldiers, kept in part because it worked well with the scenery, which dictates much of the movement. It includes the Gingerbread Doll, whose arm is ripped off (thanks to the modern miracle of hook and loop fasteners), and a quartet of mice crossing arms, holding hands, and performing a spoof of the dance for the four little swans in *Swan Lake*. Among the little white lambs that accompany the shepherd and shepherdesses in the Pastorale is one black one, again reminiscent of some productions of *Swan Lake* where there are a few black swans sprinkled among the white ones in the corps.

"It's all in the music," Nissinen says of his deliberately understated *Nutcracker*. "I wanted to give it a fresh read, with a simple expression

Angels in *The Nutcracker* at the Boston Opera House, reproduced courtesy of Live Nation, Inc. Photo by Wally Gilbert.

without the Hollywood extravaganza I inherited here. It wasn't doing justice to the art form." He's beefed up some of the choreography. "It needs to be demanding for the dancers for the forty-plus performances we often do. It needs to inspire the next generation of artists to keep it authentic."

20

The Spring 2007 Season

A Midsummer Night's Dream, February 8–18, 2007

Before Nissinen's arrival, Boston Ballet had done a version of Shakespeare's enchanting romantic comedy by Bruce Wells, a choreographer who was already on the ballet's payroll. It was acceptable, even lovely at times. It counted on the fact that Americans read Shakespeare in school and are familiar with at least the wedding march part of the Mendelssohn score. There aren't many Americans who grow up learning about choreography, so the company once again banked on name recognition. That happily coincided with selecting what Nissinen viewed as the best version extant, Balanchine's. Balanchine ballets are copyrighted, and getting permission to perform one involves approaching the Balanchine Trust, which holds the rights to most of the master's works. If the Trust decides that the company is at a high enough level to perform the piece, it sends out a stager, someone who has probably performed the work and is in any case familiar with every step of it, to set it on the company. In this case the stager was former New York City Ballet dancer Sandra Jennings, a Bostonian who knows the company well and whose mother, Jacqueline Cronsberg, teaches at the Boston Ballet School.

Every time a Balanchine ballet is performed, the program includes the following language: "Presented by agreement with The George Balanchine Trust and produced in accordance with the Balanchine Style™ and Balanchine Technique™ Service standards established and provided by the Trust." The Trust vigilantly guards the master's works to ensure that the company stays as close as possible to the original.

As a child, Balanchine had played the part of an elf in Shakespeare's play. The experience stuck with him. Decades later, he could still speak some of *Midsummer*'s lines in Russian.

Balanchine's *Midsummer,* which premiered in New York in 1962, was the first original evening-length story ballet that he choreographed in the United States. It tells the complex tale of mortals and fairies falling in love with the wrong characters until things are, predictably and delightfully, straightened out. (Poignantly, too, as when poor Bottom realizes he's only been a sort of King for a Day.)

One of Balanchine's famous axioms is "There are no mothers-in-law in ballet," meaning that it's impossible to tell complicated stories in dance. With *Midsummer,* he proved himself wrong.

The way he tells the story reverts to the way many nineteenth-century story ballets are told. Think of *Sleeping Beauty,* where the familiar tale is all sorted out before the last act, which is thereby free to focus on the pomp of a royal wedding. A large part of this scene consists of the royals parading around, wearing extravagantly long trains that billow behind them. The same structure applies to Balanchine's *Midsummer.*

The first act of the two-act ballet is packed with mortals of various ranks, plus fairies, butterflies, hounds, and horn blowers. Even on a stage the size of the Wang's, it gets fairly, and charmingly, crowded.

Among the many enchanting moments is the discovery of the Queen of the Fairies sleeping in a giant whirling shell with an iridescent pink interior. Humor isn't a quality necessarily associated with Balanchine, but *Midsummer* is filled with choreographic jokes, as when an arrow and a flower descend from the rafters with the magic potion that makes everyone fall in love with the first creature they see on awakening.

Sweetest of all, a swarm of children playing bugs at one point fall asleep all in a heap. The children in Balanchine's *Midsummer* actually have a lot more to do than the children in many *Nutcracker*s.

"New Visions," March 1–4, 2007

The world premiere of Elo's *Brake the Eyes* was one of the great opportunities of Larissa Ponomarenko's career. She used to be known as a dancer who didn't like contemporary ballets, as someone who wanted to live in the nineteenth-century realm of Petipa. Not so. In *Brake the Eyes* Elo challenged her not only to dance like an awkward mechanical doll but to speak as well. Her tutu was miked. The narrative, a collaboration between dancer and choreographer, was in Russian and was intended to be unintelligible, even to Russian speakers, in the same sense that Italian opera may often be unintelligible to Italian speakers, because the music means changing the inflection and tone of the words.

While both Elo and Ponomarenko were elusive about what exactly she was saying, both said it was nothing of earth-shattering significance, that it was ordinary fragmented observations on the order of "the air feels chilly." Fragmented describes the rest of the complex score, too, which includes passages from five works by Mozart and an electronic soundscape by Elo's partner, Nancy Euverink, who provided a hollow, thundering va-voom that accompanied Ponomarenko's talking.

Although there was a second cast behind Ponomarenko in *Brake the Eyes,* the second cast did not perform. Ponomarenko's special qualities and her language ability defined the leading role. The idea of the mix of sounds is very European and reflects Elo's background in the Nederlands Dans Theater, where mixing media is common.

As usual with Elo's work, the lighting was dark, in this case beginning with pools of light on the floor that formed a path that Ponomarenko followed. The lighting looked at first like the underside of an airplane that has just taken off. Designed by Mark Stanley and Elo, the lights are on beams that move up and down and tilt. They are part of the choreography as much as the humans are, and their hovering is somewhat menacing.

A corps of eight dancers initially stand around quietly, as if they are witnesses to Ponomarenko's actions and to her solitude, even though she does have a surprisingly lyrical duet with Sabi Varga. Their movement is an inversion of classicism, with semaphoric gestures, turned-in legs, and jagged arms. Like both earlier and contemporary choreographers, Elo uses the device of the leitmotiv to give a character identity. One of Ponomarenko's is touching an elbow to a lifted knee, as if to emphasize the parts of the body that can bend. It's yet another form of fragmentation.

A slit in the back curtain allows dancers to enter from the rear as well as the sides of the stage, and as if to acknowledge the importance of the part of the stage that is usually a mere backdrop, there's a lot of facing upstage. In another departure from tradition, Elo often has the arms, which usually follow the lead of the legs, initiate the movement.

The corps is eventually activated, with backbends that extend right down to the floor, powerful jumps, wheelbarrowlike formations, legs bicycling in the air, and a jolly section that looks almost like a chorus line. Ponomarenko remains the outsider, right up to the enigmatic ending, in which she snaps her fingers and the lights go out. Throughout much of the piece it's unclear whether her character is victim or victimizer. With that final gesture that turns out the lights, she seems the latter.

After this unusually dramatic opener—nothing here merely to settle the audience into a ballet-watching frame of mind—came Christopher Wheeldon's *Polyphonia,* a direct homage to Balanchine. *Polyphonia,* premiered by New York City Ballet in 2001, is set to rhythmically complex piano pieces by the late György Ligeti, best known for his scores for Stanley Kubrick films. A dance for four couples in leotards, it begins with their bodies silhouetted on the back curtain at an immense scale. They seem larger-than-life ghosts of themselves, and since Wheeldon has deliberately nodded to Balanchine, it's hard not to think of the master's deliberate amplification of dancers' bodies: for him, bigger was better.

Some of the most distinctive choreography is with the woman carried upside down, head toward the ground and feet pointing upward, doing battements in the air. While Wheeldon is known for his romantic bent, here his choreography stays crisp and clear, and each section has a particular emotional tone, the entire piece knit together by Ligeti's driving score. *Polyphonia,* while a satisfying work on its own, is also derivative of the great Balanchine/Stravinsky collaborations.

"New Visions" ended with Caniparoli's *Sonata for Two Pianos and Percussion,* to the Bartok score of the same name, composed in 1937, an ominous time for Eastern Europe. In the sonata, though, Bartok strikes an optimistic and even silly chord, incorporating sounds including a cuckoo. Caniparoli's choreography, premiered during Boston Ballet's 2004 season, is a direct response to the music, with memorably playful moments as when the dancers skid along the floor like children at recess.

The Wheeldon and Caniparoli pieces, both well-crafted and thoughtful responses to the deliberately difficult scores the choreographers chose, were worth seeing if not worth a detour. Nissinen knew exactly what he was getting with them. He couldn't have in the case of Elo's brand-new *Brake the Eyes.* He took a chance and got a masterful work. One out of three isn't bad.

"Classic Balanchine," May 3–6, 2007

For the "Classic Balanchine" program, Nissinen chose three winning works: *Ballo della Regina, La Valse,* and *The Four Temperaments.* They're all well-known works, no rare revivals here, but together they offered a range of the master's styles. Nissinen had been disappointed with the lukewarm response to his presentation of Bronislava Nijinska's *Les Noces* on his Russian program. Reviving *Les Noces* was a big deal, but neither Boston audiences nor the critics seemed to recognize that. So on this Balanchine program he presented three works that would further educate his public about the greatest of twentieth-century neoclassical choreographers.

There is no more touching gift that a choreographer can give a dancer than a ballet created on that dancer. Witness Ashton's gift of *La Fille mal gardée* to Alexander Grant, who travels the world staging the piece. Another instance is George Balanchine's leaving the rights to *Ballo della Regina,* the 1978 work he created for Merrill Ashley, to its star, who was one of the most brilliant technicians in Balanchine's New York City Ballet. *Ballo* is set to the act 3 ballet music from Verdi's opera *Don Carlos,* but it is, in effect, an homage to female virtuosity and especially to what a ballerina can achieve on pointe.

In her 1984 autobiography, *Dancing for Balanchine,* Ashley, who has always been good at analyzing technique, gives a fascinating description of the intricacies of working on *Ballo* with Balanchine. The choreographer himself, an accomplished musician, had made the piano reduction of the orchestral score because none had existed. The very first day of rehearsal, he gave Ashley a step that he had long had in his mind, but he had never been able to find a dancer who could do it. The ballerina is on pointe in second position, with the legs open at about 45 degrees, and jumping and turning at the same time. Ashley couldn't do it. The problem was that he didn't want her to begin the jumps with a plié, the bent knees that usually prepare the dancer to jump. Ashley was supposed to pop up into the air without any preparation, so it would be a surprise to the audience. (She never did master it.) The next surprise was a jump forward in attitude, a bent-leg position, with arms opening graciously as if saluting the audience, and this time, blessedly, with the preparatory plié. This is a traditional ending for a variation: Balanchine wanted the audience to think perhaps the fun was over. It wasn't. He then had Ashley perform a big leap of her own choice—Balanchine often allowed his dancers, especially principals, to come up with their own solutions after he gave them the gist of what he wanted. What Ashley came up with was a big leap with a backbend and arms thrown back, something she had once seen Maya Plisetskaya do. That worked. But there were additional hops on pointe to be mastered, and it wasn't only Ashley who had to work on them. All the women in the company did, because Balanchine started giving them in class every day. *Ballo* ended up with jumps that landed on pointe even if they weren't the straight-legged ones he had initially asked for.

There is a lone man in *Ballo,* Ricky Weiss in the original, Boston Ballet soloist James Whiteside partnering Lorna Feijóo on opening night in Boston. The man's variations are filled with virtuoso steps, but not to the degree of difficulty of the women's.

Right straight down through the ranks, from *Ballo*'s leading ballerina to the four soloists and the corps of twelve, everyone is challenged by having to turn on a dime, in all likelihood more quickly than they had ever done and without regrouping to change direction, for that would spoil the surprise. All this takes place in a flirty mood. The corps and soloist women are closer to chorines than classical ballet usually gets. The plot of the seldom performed ballet in *Don Carlos* involves a fisherman searching for a perfect pearl, linked there to the Queen of Spain. In Balanchine's *Ballo,* the perfect pearl is the leading ballerina.

It's a mistake to stereotype Balanchine as a maker of austere "leotard" ballets that stretch the boundaries of classicism. He had a storytelling side (*A Midsummer Night's Dream*) and a purely romantic side as well in such ballets as *La Sonnambula* and *La Valse,* the latter of which was on the "Classic Balanchine" program. Balanchine was fascinated by the hypnotic potential of the waltz, and demonstrated it in such major works as *Liebeslieder Waltzes* and the brilliantly decadent *Vienna Waltzes.*

In choreographing this two-part piece to Ravel's *Valses nobles et sentimentales* and *La Valse,* he created an essay in doom. Each of the eight waltzes in the first part has its own mood, from frivolous to macabre. To me, these first waltzes read as a warm-up to the real thing. You would be disappointed to have the ballet end with them.

Francia Russell was the répétiteur who staged *La Valse* for Boston, and in rehearsal she urged the dancers to "Throw yourself around! This is a BIG waltz!" To one dancer she said in a tone of mock accusation, "You were taught to be *precise,* weren't you?" as if precision were a sin. The semblance of precision isn't what's wanted in *La Valse,* and indeed, Russell got the dancers to inflate their movements to fill the Ballet's Grand Studio so fully that a visitor was tempted to duck behind a chair to avoid injury inflicted by a flying ballerina. The whirling is punctuated by flinging arms and flicking wrists, all meant to create a sense of recklessness that is hard for classically trained dancers to master—or at least for those who didn't grow up with Balanchine. But underneath the recklessness there is, of course, precision; otherwise, the dancers run the risk of spinning into each other. As Russell put it, "You definitely have to be in the right place at the right time in this ballet. Otherwise you're toast."

The first half of the ballet establishes a foreboding anticipation that is realized in the second, which has a plot line about a woman who finally succumbs to the figure of Death, lured away from the mortal partner she had just danced with. The woman, all in white, is sometimes played as an innocent young girl, sometimes as a mature sophisticate. Her arm gestures are insistent, as if she's trying to tell the story of a troubled relationship. She is seduced by Death's costuming her in black, right before the audience's eyes. The transformation, if well done, is shocking. And "well done" involves still more precision. If the black diamond necklace isn't fastened in a second, if the long black gloves don't slide easily over the white ones, if the ballerina's elbows don't glide smoothly through the sleeves of the black coat, the effect is ruined. Finally, Death holds up a broken mirror for the woman who was formerly in white to inspect herself. Suddenly she realizes she is doomed.

"Classic Balanchine" closed with the 1946 *The Four Temperaments.* Set to a commissioned score by Hindemith, it is a landmark, a starkly beautiful precursor of such works as *Agon* but with no obvious predecessors. Balanchine used the Hindemith as a springboard for a new vocabulary of dance. Hindemith composed a three-part theme with a quartet of variations named for the four temperaments of medieval medicine: Melancholic, Sanguinic, Phlegmatic, and Choleric. In Balanchine's choreography and Hindemith's score those translate roughly to pensive, confident, impassive, and angry. But it's best not to take these adjectives too literally. Balanchine used the three themes to set out his vocabulary,

Larissa Ponomarenko and Yury Yanowsky with Anthony Randazzo, rehearsing George Balanchine's *La Valse,* choreography by George Balanchine, © The George Balanchine Trust. Photo by Wally Gilbert.

to offer, one by one, the essentials of classical dance. Then, in the variations, he elaborated on the themes, warping and twisting the steps in ways that had never been attempted before.

In *The Four Temperaments,* hips are deliberately thrown out of direct alignment with the shoulders, dancers bourrée in a hunched over, predatory position, like insects on the prowl, and some of the angled arm positions suggest Egyptian art or perhaps the antiquity of Nijinsky's *L'Après-midi d'un faune.* Bart Cook, a former City Ballet dancer now turned répétiteur, worked with the Boston dancers on the piece. Some of his points were subtle. "Don't broadcast that it's a pas de deux," he told two dancers. "Just come out on stage." His instructions echoed Balanchine's famous maxim, "Just dance." In other words, don't announce your presence. Cook got the dancers through the off-balance partnering that is another Balanchine hallmark, and those partnered pirouettes in which the ballerina's standing leg is bent are another instance of Balanchine trying an old step in a new, eye-catching way.

"When I first did The *Four Temperaments,* it had been out of the repertory for a decade," Cook says. "So it was almost a new ballet. There was a dilemma about which version of the ending to do. There were four different ones."

New York City Ballet continues to be a workshop, Cook says. Balanchine himself changed his works over the years, sometimes drastically, either to suit himself or to suit a particular dancer. Cook is of the camp that believes that Balanchine's works shouldn't be frozen, that there should be some leeway in staging them. The ending of choice? It's a series of sweeping, tidal lifts, in which the women soar above the stage in huge arcs. Says Cook, "I think of it as a prayer."

Giselle, May 10–20, 2007

Maina Gielgud's production of *Giselle* closed Boston Ballet's 2006–07 season. Gielgud had first taught her version of the classic to the company in 2002. *Giselle* is the work she has set more than any other. She has also danced both leading roles, the fragile heroine and the frigid man-hating Myrtha, queen of the wilis.

Premiered at the Paris Opera on June 28, 1841, *Giselle* is the quintessential Romantic ballet. It was not, however, the first. That honor, it is generally acknowledged, goes to the third act ballet from Meyerbeer's

John Lam, Kelsey Hellebuyck, Krista Ettlinger, Claire Stallman, and Luciana Voltolini in *Melancholic* from George Balanchine's *The Four Temperaments*, choreography by George Balanchine, © The George Balanchine Trust, at the Auditorio Conde Duque in Madrid. Photo by Wally Gilbert.

opera *Robert le Diable,* which debuted a decade earlier, also at the Paris Opera. This featured dead nuns rising from their graves, precursors of the wilis in *Giselle,* who are maidens betrayed by men before their wedding day. The wilis also rise from their graves at night, to dance to death any man who enters their dark forest.

It is largely due to the composer Adolphe Adam that *Giselle* has earned an enduring role in the ballet repertory. Adam's sophisticated use of leitmotifs to help define characters and moods anticipated such composers as Tchaikovsky and Wagner by several decades.

In the ballet's debut, the choreography was credited to Jean Coralli, official ballet master of the Paris Opera. Jules Perrot, a ballet master who became the lover of Carlotta Grisi, the first Giselle, and also in effect her manager, probably had a hand in the choreography as well, and nowadays he is generally credited along with Perrot. As for the scenario, it started with a story by the poet Heinrich Heine, who in-

spired another poet, Théophile Gautier (who was also a ballet critic), to create a complex plot for *Giselle*. The popular playwright Jules-Henri Vernoy de Saint-Georges simplified Gautier's version to the point of comprehension.

Boston's program cautiously noted that the choreography was "after Jean Coralli, Jules Perrot, and Marius Petipa." Petipa added to the original choreography in 1848. Two years earlier, the Philadelphia-born pioneering American ballerina Mary Ann Lee had staged a *Giselle* in Boston, after studying in Paris with Coralli himself. The ballet was such a hit that it spread across the Atlantic within five years of its Paris debut.

Giselle's plot is kindergarten, but the product has to be graduate school, something that balletomanes can ponder no matter how many times they have seen it. The ballet takes place in a Rhineland village during harvest time. Giselle is a peasant girl with a heart murmur. She is in love with Albrecht, a nobleman who has disguised himself as a peasant in order to flirt with her. His rival, Hilarion, a real peasant, figures out Albrecht's true identity and reveals it when an aristocratic hunting party that includes Albrecht's fiancée shows up in the village. Giselle's heart condition takes on an emotional as well as a physical aspect, and this double whammy leads to the most famous mad scene in ballet (and the reason *Giselle* is often called "the ballerina's *Hamlet*") and then to the protagonist's death. End of act 1.

Act 2 opens in a dark forest ruled by Myrtha, queen of the wilis, who summons the other wilis from their graves. Hilarion appears. The wilis literally dance him to death. Albrecht's appearance is more prolonged. Giselle, as elusive in death as she had been eager in life, flits through the remorseful Albrecht's presence. Now he sees her; now he doesn't. Finally they dance a last, sad duet. Giselle pleads with Myrtha to let Albrecht live, but the Queen is relentless. Giselle's procrastination saves him, though. A church bell signals the arrival of dawn, when the wilis, including Giselle, must retreat to their graves, leaving the desolate Albrecht alone onstage.

Not surprisingly, because she comes both from the land of Shakespeare and from theatrical royalty, Gielgud is passionate and demanding about acting in ballet. "I like to start by talking with one leading couple at a time," she says. "With the first act, we talk about how long Giselle and Albrecht have known each other. How long has Wilfred [Albrecht's loyal servant] been in his master's employ? What was the weather like when Albrecht walked to Giselle's grave? What was he thinking about the awful thing he had done? Things like that. I do something similar even with the corps. It's important that they understand that they're not part of the scenery."

Gielgud's staging emphasizes clarity and continuity. If you see it several times, you begin to think about it the way she does, that there is nothing there without a meaning. Take the peasant pas de deux in the first act. This virtuoso duet is for two happy, healthy people, well suited to each other in terms of class, as opposed to Giselle and Albrecht. We don't find out anything else about them. To a first-time viewer of *Giselle,* this piece can seem like filler, to give the leads a breather. But they also serve as a foil to Giselle and Albrecht, whose relationship is so complex and ends so tragically.

It is up to each ballerina playing Giselle to decide how much to emphasize the character's heart problem. The most successful ones are subtle, using an occasional sign of faintness or placing a hand over the heart to indicate the condition. Anything more deflects from the effectiveness of the mad scene and can seem melodramatic.

The choreography of *Giselle* is as prescient as its score, especially in the second act. The long diagonal line that the wilis form to hurtle men to their deaths prefigures the choreography of both the second and fourth acts of *Swan Lake* and even the abstract works of Balanchine a century after that.

Myrtha's first entrance doesn't necessarily look difficult, but its sheer nakedness makes it nerve-racking for the ballerina, who steps onstage and into a long arabesque that silhouettes her against the backdrop. It's an unforgiving position. If her supporting foot wiggles at all, the intent of the pose, to convey absolute supernatural authority, is ruined. She holds the arabesque during a promenade—a slow turn made possible by lifting the heel of the supporting foot in miniscule doses that are ideally unseen. They mustn't look lumpy. The effect must be that she turns through some magical power. Finally, having rotated a complete 360 degrees, she's back where she began, and she dips into a deep penché, tilting her torso forward while lifting the back leg. In some flashier virtuoso phrases in ballet, there are ways to mask a botched step. In Myrtha's entrance, there aren't.

The same is true of Giselle's own second act entrance. She quietly slips from her grave and walks hesitantly toward Myrtha, eyes cast down, before exploding into a series of superfast hops in a circle, in arabesque. But these hops are performed backward, counterclockwise, creating a sense of disorientation, as if Giselle wanted to turn back time, to unravel the plot that has led to her death. She then launches into a series of jumps that look as if she is propelled by another power. Surely this frail maiden granted a brief reprieve from death couldn't perform them on her own.

The wilis, too, have a dramatic series of hops in arabesque. Traveling in lines that pass each other, they end up on the other side of the stage from where they began. Those who started on the right reach the left, and the reverse. They move as if they're unconscious, tilting forward from the waist, and their hops have to be soft so as not to appear strained. They are, after all, ghosts. While the first act of *Giselle* can seem quaint, the second act remains a chilling masterpiece.

Ponomarenko, who played the lead in Boston's *Giselle* on opening night in 2002, has the fragile looks and soft movement to make her a perfect candidate for the work. On Gielgud's style of coaching, Ponomarenko says, "Ten years ago I would have cried in her rehearsals. They're so detailed. But now I'm used to that level of detail, because we had Tatiana Legat here and she works the same way, with endless corrections. I was looking forward to Maina coming back. Maina has been around the world with various companies. She has a great sense of theatrical tradition."

One technical problem the Russian-trained Ponomarenko had with Gielgud's *Giselle* was with port de bras, or carriage of the arms. "Russians expand their souls through bigger arms," Ponomarenko explains. "The British are more reserved. Maina's port de bras are simpler. It's a very different approach, one that was hard for me. I worked at it in the studio. But in the dress rehearsal Mikko was watching me with a microphone in his hand, and he kept saying, 'Lower your arms.'" Nineteenth-century prints indicate that the original arms were low and rounded, the upper body tilted forward from the waist, and also that the legs weren't lifted above waist height. No self-respecting twenty-first-century ballerina who has worked assiduously to develop an extension that brings her foot into the vicinity of her head is happy with this lower extension, and so Ponomarenko's legs flew up, but they did so with the ease of a bird's wings. Just as Ponomarenko's second act entrance saw her go from hesitant steps to those madly whirling turns, so her Albrecht, the Russian dancer Roman Rykine, entered slowly, his long black cape trailing behind him until he started to run, when it billowed behind him, a symbol perhaps of his desperate state of mind.

The 2006–07 season had been one of the toughest ever for the company, not just financially but also in terms of the repertoire Nissinen had thrown at the dancers. After the last performance of *Giselle,* also the last of the season, one young woman who had been a wili came backstage and immediately plunked herself down on the floor, unable even to make it down to the dressing rooms. She gingerly removed the toe shoes from her blistered feet, with every inflamed toe individually wrapped. "That hurt so much," she said to no one in particular, "that I was thinking maybe I wouldn't point my toes." But she had.

21

The Spanish Tour

Ballet companies need to tour. Performing for different audiences, on different stages, refreshes dancers. It wakes them up and shakes them out of whatever hometown rut they may have fallen into. They get the opinions of other critics in other cities, and if the reviews are positive, they arrive back home as conquering heroes.

Nissinen's biggest accomplishment of the 2006–07 season was a six-week, seven-venue tour of Spain, where the troupe appeared at the festivals that are such a popular fixture of Spanish summer life. He had been itching for the company to get out of Boston, to visit places that might appreciate his dancers more than the home crowd did. The last time the company had had a foreign tour was 1991.

I caught up with them in Madrid, midway through the tour, where they danced for four nights at the Auditorio Conde Duque, an outdoor theater set up every summer for the Festival Veranos de la Villa. In the close quarters of the Auditorio Conde Duque I found myself noticing details I hadn't when watching the company in the Wang. Gestures seemed sharper, brighter, more focused. It was difficult to tell whether this was because the dancers were so excited at being in a foreign country or whether that brightness had been there all along, just obscured by their usual theater. There was also a downside. Seeing *Serenade* outdoors when there was still a bit of daylight robbed it of some of its nocturnal magic. The opening had a bleached-out look. Pigeons squealed overhead, as if they wanted to join in. You don't get that unwelcome distraction in an indoor theater. (This was, however, a reminder that the first performance of *Serenade* had been on an outdoor stage.) Despite the heat, the sun, and the pigeons, the Boston dancers' reading of this venerable icon was superb. As the Russian Girl, Kathleen Breen Combes danced not only with precision but also with the appearance of spontaneity, as if she were making up the part as she went along. I had never seen the role performed better.

The Auditorio Conde Duque proved to be a fine, if informal, setting for the performances. The stage and the bleacher seating are in the courtyard of what had been a huge brick military compound. The shows didn't get under way until 9:30, when the sun was just going down and the ovenlike heat was subsiding. But the dancers had to rehearse all day in 100 degree temperatures, and even at 9:30 the heat seemed trapped in the box of the proscenium stage. It didn't help that in *La Sylphide*, which is set in the highlands of Scotland, the male dancers had to wear woolen kilts, while the dancer playing the mother of James, the story's male protagonist, was kitted out in a floor-length woolen turtleneck dress. Still, "dancers much prefer heat to cold," Nissinen noted. "It keeps them limber and loose and less prone to injury." (He, meanwhile, was wearing a cool open-necked shirt and cotton trousers.)

The Spanish presenter, Ada Casanovas, was in attendance before, during, and after performances and rehearsals, looking remarkably calm given the massive responsibilities of a tour and the hundreds of things that could go wrong.

It was Casanovas who asked for the kind of repertory that Boston brought to Spain: August Bournonville's 1836 *La Sylphide* and a Balanchine triple bill consisting of *Serenade, The Four Temperaments,* and an abbreviated "concert" version of *Who Cares?* Generally, performances were sold out, and the mayors in various cities showed up for the shows.

Still, the repertory was more traditional fare than Nissinen wanted to present. "I wanted to show Jorma's work, and Mark Morris's, and the way we perform Jiři Kylián and Christopher Wheeldon. We could have ignited the fire even more." Next time. In Madrid, Casanovas was so pleased with the way the performances were going that she was talking about bringing the company back every other year.

There was another reason for the repertory in the two programs: they were ready to go. Boston had already performed *Serenade* and *The Four Temperaments* a few months earlier, and *Sylphide* was set to open in the

Yury Yanowsky in *La Sylphide* at the Auditorio Conde Duque in Madrid. Photo by Wally Gilbert.

fall 2007 season. So the company wouldn't have to incur the expense of additional rehearsal weeks.

There were a few injuries on the tour. Although there was nothing in the career-ending category, they did keep company physical therapist Michelina Cassella busy in her makeshift PT headquarters backstage. "Generally, when the dancers are in the theater, I'm in the theater," said Cassella, who is more experienced at touring than most of the Boston dancers. She's done it with the Alvin Ailey American Dance Theater and London's Royal Ballet. "Some of our young ones have never been out of the country before," she said. Roughly 80 percent of the company had never been on tour. Feijóo, though, is a veteran of touring, especially in Spain. "When I was with the Cuban ballet, we had come to Spain every summer," she said. "I have a lot of friends here." Her fan club was out in full force for her Madrid shows.

Cassella talked while massaging Feijóo's aching calves and sore feet and looking at the X-rays that principal dancer Nelson Madrigal, Feijóo's husband, had just had taken at a local hospital. Feijoo complained that her legs ached because the stage floor in Tenerife, the first stop on the tour, had been too hard.

"There's enormous pressure on the medical person when a company is on tour," Cassella said, adding that before she left Boston, Dr. Lyle Micheli, the company's physician, had given her the names and telephone numbers of doctors in each area of Spain where the company was traveling, should anything truly extreme happen. Nothing did.

Before leaving Boston, Cassella had to pack. In addition to her own clothes, "which I packed and unpacked seventeen times in Spain, so I don't want to go on tour again anytime soon," she had the entire triage unit to squeeze into an enormous crate with double doors. "We took every kind of knee brace, ankle brace, blood pressure unit, thermometers, and all kinds of other stuff, including our treatment table and thousands of antiseptic wipes. I have a list a mile long of everything I brought. I tried to keep everything as clean and sterile as we do at the clinic in Boston. But when you're on tour, you don't even always have access to a sink. So I took gallons of hand sanitizer. In Las Palmas there were portable potties, and you know how they are. So the dancers were apologizing to me for coming all the time to ask for hand sanitizers, but I thought that was great. Hydration, rest, and sanitation are the keys to staying healthy on tour. We had only a couple of dancers who were ill,

and they were just out for a day or two. Before the tour we had meet-ings with them about bringing sunscreen. After all, it's Spain. We didn't have anyone get a sunburn," Cassella says. "You can't have a sylph with a sunburn."

The dancers' reactions to the tour varied according to how long they had been in the ballet business. Brittany Summer, a teenager who had just joined Boston Ballet II, was ecstatic. "It's been unreal," she said. "I had been to Italy for a vacation with my family, so this was my second time out of the country. I joined BB II in June, and I started rehearsing for the tour. I was just an understudy, in case something went wrong." Something did. Another dancer scheduled to dance in *The Four Tem-peraments* fell ill, and Summer got to perform in the Melancholic section of the work, as one of the four "kicking" girls who enter so aggressively. It was another case of Nissinen's maxim, "One dancer's injury is another dancer's opportunity."

John Lam, Kathleen Breen Combes, and Melanie Atkins in *La Sylphide* at the Auditorio Conde Duque in Madrid. Photo by Wally Gilbert.

Summer didn't get to perform in *La Sylphide,* however. "Most of the corps girls have been pretty healthy," she says, with no sign of regret in her voice. "*La Sylphide* doesn't have that much high-impact dancing for the corps, but there's a lot of jumping for the principals."

She quickly learned the touring regime. "All of our hotels were nice," she said. "We got a per diem to cover meals and other daily expenses. It varied in each city. The biggest one was in Madrid, where we got $144 a day." (The dancers' contract calls for their per diem on tour to match that of the U.S. government.) "In all the hotels our breakfast was included. The hotel in Madrid had champagne for breakfast, but I didn't see any of the dancers drinking any. Usually people grabbed a couple of pieces of fruit from the buffet for later on. It was hard to get used to the eating schedule. People in Spain don't start eating dinner until 9 p.m., and you can still eat at midnight. When we got to each city we had a day off, so we could go to the beach or do something like take a train to Barcelona and look at the buildings."

She learned the rules of curtain calls. "The shows were extremely well received," she said. "At the end of every show, there were individual curtain calls for the principals and then a full company call. If there was enough applause, there would be another curtain call. It's determined by the lights onstage. If they kept the lights on, then we knew to walk forward and take another bow. We did that until the applause really died down and the lights dimmed. Then we knew that the curtain calls were over."

"The accommodations have been great," says soloist Melanie Atkins, who toured for several years with Miami City Ballet before she moved to Boston. For principal dancers there are five single rooms. That's in the AGMA (American Guild of Musical Artists) contract. "But because there are so many couples on the tour, those rooms trickle down to the soloists. Soloists and corps dancers choose their own roommates. It's not like a freshman college dorm where you have to share with someone you've never met. The accommodations in the first couple of venues were five star. They took a dive in Madrid, where they were, well, basic."

Unless you're a first-time teenager and it's better than summer camp, touring is grueling. Each venue's stage on the Spanish tour was a different size and shape, which meant that the dancers and ballet masters had to readjust the choreography to fit each one, requiring many hours of rehearsal in each city. The rehearsing never let up. The production staff's work was endless, too. Production manager Benjamin Phillips and his staff had only one day off during the six-week tour. It was well after midnight when wardrobe manager Charles Heightchew would finish sorting tights and other practice and performance wear into bags labeled with each dancer's name, so it could all be sent out to a laundry and readied for the next evening. When the costumes had to be transferred from Tenerife to Las Palmas, they were put onto a refrigerated produce truck on a ferry. They arrived nice and cool but, alas, with enough time to heat up before the evening show. Touring inevitably involves glitches. The personal laundry of two production team members, Nate Noce and Karim Badwan, was held hostage in Las Palmas because the laundromat to which they had entrusted everything in their suitcases closed early and didn't reopen until the following day, after the company had left the island. The two had to buy new wardrobes to last them for the next few days. Fortunately, Carmen Robles, the mother of principal dancer Yury Yanowsky, lives on Las Palmas, and she managed to deliver the clean laundry to Madrid within the week.

The misadventures of the musical scores were more dramatic. Jonathan McPhee had shipped the scores in plenty of time for their arrival in Spain. But vigilant Spanish customs authorities decided to take all the scores apart, in case the bindings held any dangerous substances. They left the dismantled scores in a heap instead of reassembling them. Pages of music by Herman Lovenskjold (*Sylphide*), Hindemith (*Four T's*), Gershwin (*Who Cares?*), and Tchaikovsky (*Serenade*) were scrambled together. No doubt there is some adventurous contemporary choreographer who would enjoy tackling a score made up of a page of Hindemith next to a page of Lovenskjold, but this tour wasn't the moment for it. McPhee had to resend the scores.

The scores were needed for only three performances. For financial reasons, the other fifteen were danced to taped music, which, in the Madrid performances I saw, inevitably dampened the liveliness and immediacy of the event. McPhee flew back and forth to conduct the three live performances, but the Boston Ballet orchestra didn't go with him. Tenerife hired Orquesta Sinfónica de Tenerife and the Santander Festival hired the Lithuanian National Orchestra to accompany the performances. Eastern European orchestras are relatively inexpensive to import, McPhee says. However, "the Lithuanians had never played for

Melanie Atkins and Yury Yanowsky in *La Sylphide* at the Auditorio Conde Duque in Madrid. Photo by Wally Gilbert.

ballet, and they usually don't play in a pit. So they were a little stiff." That said, McPhee, who has conducted for dance companies all over the world, predicted, "It's great that Boston Ballet is touring now. The benefits are going to be visible next season."

He was talking about benefits visible onstage. There are others as well, including company bonding. In Boston, the dancers take class, rehearse, and perform together, and then disperse to their individual homes, some in the South End where the company is headquartered, others in Boston suburbs. On tour, they're together virtually twenty-four hours a day, eating and sleeping in the same restaurants and hotels. Although several of them are native Spanish speakers, for most there was also the language barrier that brought the non-Spanish speakers even closer together. The foreign venues refreshed not only the dancers but also the Bostonians following the company on a fund-raising donor trip. It's Nissinen's hope that donors sharing such a foreign experience with the company will increase their commitment to it and thereby their donations.

No one worked harder on the tour than Nissinen. It was sometimes 4 a.m. before he and the crew stopped tinkering with the lighting, which never seemed to satisfy him, and on more than one occasion he pulled an all-nighter. He also had to keep the dancers calm and motivated. Before one performance he spent an hour in the wings listening to a dancer who was upset about casting. "He felt he wasn't getting enough performances and the roles he wanted," Nissinen said later. "I can't really change that, but at least I can talk to him about it." There were a couple of dancers who developed medical problems and were sent home by Nissinen. Halfway through the tour, after Madrid, "I had to send Larissa Ponomarenko home because she had a bad case of tendinitis and couldn't dance," Nissinen said. "And I had to send another girl home because she was getting too thin." Although less of a problem than it was in the past, anorexia remains an issue for ballet companies, and Boston is vigilant in guarding against it.

Serenade and *The Four Temperaments* are undisputed masterpieces. *Who Cares?* is Balanchine pop, a reminder that Mr. B. worked on Broadway, in the movies, and even in a circus, choreographing for elephants. No snob he. *Who Cares?* debuted in 1970, around the time when American modern dance choreographers, not previously known for their lightheartedness, were starting to use pop music. Twyla Tharp's landmark *Deuce Coupe,* set to music by the Beach Boys, debuted in 1973. In reviewing *Who Cares?* critic Nancy Goldner noted that Balanchine "talks about Bob Hope and Westerns and has used Gershwin songs for his newest ballet simply because he loves them all. He loves America. . . . It is not camp, nor is Balanchine going slumming or being whimsical when he choreographs to cowboy tunes and Gershwin." However, not all Europeans are Balanchine fans. In the chatty diary that Nissinen posted on Boston Ballet's Web site, he noted that ticket sales for the second performance in Tenerife—the first stop on the tour, where two performances of the "Classic Balanchine" program had been scheduled—were slow, and so the second performance was switched to *La Sylphide.*

The Boston dancers who performed *Who Cares?* in Madrid were all born after Balanchine made the work. For them, there was nothing radical about the combination of Gershwin and Balanchine. (The most revolutionary thing they had done in 2007, in my view, was Nijinska's 1923 *Les Noces*.) They grew up with a mix of pop music and classical dance—Tharp is also in the company's repertory—and their ease with the material in *Who Cares?* was evident. "I've done that role for a number of years," says Atkins, who danced to "I'll Build a Stairway to Paradise," "I Got Rhythm," and "Who Cares?" "The Spanish audiences really enjoyed it," she says, "because it's so American. It's fun, and it looks easy, although it's one of the most difficult ballets to dance." The concert version that Boston performs uses just four dancers. "If all four aren't really selling it, it brings the whole performance down," Atkins says. "You have to be 120 percent all the time. We've had fun with it. We push each other. I performed it with both casts in Madrid. The pas de deux is very flirty, and Yury Yanowsky and Carlos Molina have totally different takes on it. Yury is very suave, and Carlos is rambunctious. I'm so familiar with this ballet that I have to try not to let it get stale. So I don't always look at my partner the same way, and I use different arms, different heads. Mikko really encourages that."

The dancers had to expend more conscious effort on mastering the style of *La Sylphide* than they had in the Balanchine works. They had been coached in *Sylphide* back in Boston by Sorella Englund, the Royal Danish Ballet star who excelled as the Sylph and then graduated into the part of Madge, the witch. (Like Nissinen and Elo, Englund was born a Finn.) Some of the dancers obviously had to remind themselves to switch their posture from the pulled-up, ready-to-go-anywhere stance of Balanchine to the softer lines of Bournonville's choreography, with its gracious tilt forward from the waist, filigree footwork, and ingratiating demeanor. One of the things that makes you really care about the Sylph is that she is so innocent and playful, clapping her hands and gently jumping.

The original *Sylphide* was choreographed in 1832 by Filippo Taglioni, who was determined to make a star out of his daughter Marie. Lincoln Kirstein writes that "*La Sylphide* established the mystique of the ballerina. Famous dancers, from Dupré to Vestris, were Gods of the Dance; no ballerina had been hailed as Priestess, and Taglioni now assumed that title." Kirstein also notes that the father's "corrective port de bras for his long-armed daughter became part of canonical instruction." Marie was possessed of simian arms; her father rounded them to make them look shorter and further minimized their length through *Sylphide*'s signature poses, including the coy forefinger under the chin with both elbows bent.

Sylphide's plot—a mortal man falls in love with a supernatural being he cannot possess physically—is repeated, with variations, in Romantic ballets including *Giselle,* in later classics including *Swan Lake,* and even, at a stretch, in *Serenade,* which, while plotless, has a whiff of narrative. Hence the names "Russian Dancer" and "Dark Angel," which have come to be associated with the leading female roles. All these ballets conclude with the female protagonist disappearing (unless it's in one of those happy-ending *Swan Lake*s), and the endings of *Sylphide* and *Serenade* are eerily similar, with the leading ballerinas being solemnly carried offstage.

Boston Ballet presented two Sylphs in Madrid: Feijóo and Erica Cornejo. Both demonstrated a full understanding of the untouchable, virginal quality of the role, although Cornejo gave a more subdued interpretation of it, perhaps due to an irritated hip. Feijóo, raised in the Russo-Cuban style of Romantic ballet, which is florid and dramatic, played up the emotions in the part. She was all flirtatious innocence in the beginning, and she made viewers believe that she really could fly up the chimney unaided and twine herself around a tree like a vine. Every bone in her body seemed to curl. Her jump was effortless, weightless. When in a remorseful state, her fingers became streams of tears and her bourrées trembled with sadness. Her James, Yury Yanowsky, was suitably confused, torn between an apparition he desperately desired and a more mundane life with his fiancée, Effie. Englund has said that she thinks "James is one of those incredibly sensitive souls who just can't imagine getting married to a good solid girl, having lots of kids, and becoming a good farmer with lots of animals. For him that would be death. That's why he created the Sylph. She represents his escape to something else." In Englund's interpretation, the Sylph doesn't even exist as a supernatural creature, only as a figment of James's imagination.

The third main character in *La Sylphide* is Madge, a witch and, in some productions, a fortune-teller with a grudge against James. Madge gives James the scarf that he wraps around the Sylph's arms, not knowing that this would make her wings drop off and kill her. Elizabeth Olds, a former principal dancer with Canada's Royal Winnipeg Ballet, is Nissinen's assistant, but he and Englund selected her and Atkins as Madge for the tour. (Former New York City Ballet star Merrill Ashley, who had also been coached by Englund in the role of Madge and had danced it in Boston, had wanted to come on the tour, but the company couldn't afford to bring her.) Olds made it a three-fer by also acting as the PR representative. Englund is eloquent and inventive in her thoughts on Madge, whom she does not see as the classic crone but, at various stages of playing the role, as everything from a bird to a bag lady.

"Sorella does not want Madge to be an old hag, and she requested specifically that the makeup not portray her that way," said Olds. "Madge is crippled in some way: Her disability can be personalized to suit the artist, and she's been taunted or shunned because of it. So while working with Sorella I needed to establish my own personal disability/limp/crippled physical part to make her my own. I experimented with various limps, feet issues, and so on, before trying out sort of a hip-hitch thing that affected my walk in a certain way. When she saw that, Sorella said she felt that the hip thing worked best for me, because it was kind of sexy. Madge was likely a beautiful woman at some point in her life, and then people and life were cruel to her."

At the end of both *Sylphide* performances in Madrid, the leading dancers got the standing ovations they deserved. The audience even put down the fans they had used to cool themselves during the performance in order to clap. Indeed, the Spanish audiences and theaters were uniformly hospitable, Nissinen said, giving the Boston dancers the kind of appreciative welcome they don't get back home. He noted that in Las Palmas, the company's second stop, "Every ticket to Boston Ballet cost 10 Euros [about $13 then], because the performances were subsidized by the city." Hanging in the air was his frustration over the lack of city support back in Boston, even though, in his view, "by continuing to tour we could be a great ambassador for the city."

Nissinen feels that his company was "amazing in *Serenade* and *The Four T's,*" and while there's a bit of boasting in Nissinen's makeup, this time I would concur. "I would be proud to take that program to the Paris Opera or anywhere else in the world," he says. Nissinen is ambitious, optimistic, and full of grand plans no matter how dire the company's financial situation. Some of those plans come to fruition; others don't. Sitting on the bleachers in Madrid while his dancers sweat through the company class that begins their work day (at 6 p.m. in this case), he mentions the possibility of bringing the troupe to La Scala, with Balanchine's *Ballo della Regina* on one of the programs, an appropriate choice given that *Ballo* is set to music by Verdi.

The public relations benefits of the six weeks in Spain weren't all they could have been in Boston, partly because the Spanish tour coincided with a particularly rocky moment in the company's administration, which was being restructured. Shortly before the tour began, the two people in the Ballet's PR office left, leaving the Ballet to hire a New York PR firm to fill in. The age of computers, though, meant that the company could generate its own publicity, in the form of dancers' blogs posted online, some of them picked up and published by the *Boston Globe.* A decade or two ago, the *Globe* would have automatically sent a critic on the tour to witness and evaluate what went on firsthand instead of relying on sunny reports from a company member. "Touring," says Melanie Atkins, "gets the name out there. You would have thought we would get more press at home." Corps dancer Sarah Wroth was the author of one of the blogs. In Madrid, she wrote about the heat and about a stagehand washing the floor. "As the mop passed over the floor, the trail of cleanser left a streak of wet that only lasted a second in the dry heat before baking away in the breeze. My lungs burned two nights ago after a booming dress rehearsal of *Serenade.* Thank goodness for cardiovascular cross training, or I might have ended up falling in a pale blue puddle on the floor."

Wroth also wrote about the surprising lack of dinner opportunities after shows that generally ended after midnight. Spaniards may start eating dinner at 9 p.m., but, Wroth lamented, they shut their doors by 12:30. "In every city, so far, a large group of dancers will discover one particular after-show establishment, the owner of which will receive at least twenty dancers' worth of business right at closing time. Most owners we have met were happy to unload all the leftover food for the day on the ravenous dancers."

The press the company got in Spain was generally positive if not downright rapturous. The headline in the arts section of the August 16 edition of *El Pais,* Spain's leading national newspaper, read, "Eternal Love with Absolute Virtuosity—Boston Ballet Dazzles in the Perelada Festival with Their Version of *La Sylphide.*" Another major newspaper, *El Periodico,* ran this headline: "The Embodiment of Romanticism—

Boston Ballet Offers a Virtuoso, Energetic, and Brilliant Version of the Classic *La Sylphide.*"

The queen of Spain turned up for the August 18 performance of *La Sylphide* in Palma de Mallorca. The dancers' reaction to seeing her backstage after the performance varied in the same way that their reaction to the whole tour did. Summer was thrilled. "She had all these assistants who let us know when she was coming and what she would be doing. Mostly we were just standing around, but she talked to a few of the principals."

"The protocol was don't touch her until she touches you," Atkins said. "She came with a bunch of her grandchildren, who were afraid of me because they had just seen me dance the witch onstage and I was still in costume. They were a little shy. It was like Halloween for them." Olds was more blasé about the backstage royalty thing. "Queen Sofia is my seventh or eighth royal. The list includes Queen Elizabeth, Princess Anne, Prince Edward, Prince Takamoto . . ."

At the end of the six weeks in Spain—unusually long for a ballet tour these days—Nissinen said that he and the dancers were not so much exhausted as exhilarated and looking forward to their next excursion out of Boston. By that time Nissinen had three invitations to return to festivals in Spain in 2009, and he wrote in his online letter back home, "Our stock value has definitely gone up, and future tours in Europe should now be easier for us."

After the close of its spring 2008 season in Boston, the company had engagements to perform both at the Spoleto Festival USA in Charleston, South Carolina, and at the Kennedy Center in Washington, D.C., as part of the Ballet Across America series. And Nissinen had a contract to tour Korea in September of that year, before the start of the fall season. His goal of getting the company out and about was being achieved.

22

Accomplishment & Uncertainty

Despite Boston Ballet's ongoing financial problems, 2006 and 2007 were years in which the company's steady improvement began to be recognized. Twice in 2007 the company made the cover of *Dance* magazine, America's best known dance publication. Jorma Elo was April's cover, and soloist Kathleen Breen Combes graced October's cover in a pose from Elo's *Brake the Eyes.* In the article about Combes, Elo lauded her for being "willing to try everything, even if I have crazy ideas."

"I Brake for Boston Ballet" was the headline on a September 2007 blog by Wendy Perron, the editor in chief of *Dance.* Perron praised the program the company had brought to the Guggenheim Museum in New York that month, part of the museum's Works & Process series. The repertory was daring, with excerpts from Jorma Elo's *Brake the Eyes,* Helen Pickett's *Etesian,* and, somewhat incongruously, the White Swan pas de deux. Perron particularly liked the dancing of Larissa Ponomarenko, "who carried off a sublime Odette," she wrote, as well as being the lead in Elo's *Brake the Eyes.* It's hard to imagine two more disparate ballets. But Boston Ballet, to Perron's expert eye, pulled them off.

Perron rightly credited Nissinen with the sudden Jorma Elo trend in this country. "None of us had heard of him before Mikko brought him to Boston as resident choreographer," she says. "But now he is everywhere, setting and making works on companies across the United States and Europe. I like it that not every work of his is a masterpiece. He's still experimenting. What's exciting is his wild movement coupled with a sure sense of form." At the Guggenheim appearance, excerpts from

Pickett's *Etesian* were danced by Combes, who, says Perron, "makes Forsythe-type movements into something long and lyrical and limpid."

Other dancers stood out, Perron says. "For example, the sharp and forceful Rie Ichikawa. I've recently seen the company a couple of times in Boston, and the overall level is excellent. So the upshot is that Boston Ballet seems to be succeeding in blazing a new path as it also maintains ballet history. Bravo!"

Perron says that she saw Boston Ballet many years ago, and she wasn't terribly impressed. She saw Elo's *Plan to B* in the "Fall for Dance" series at New York's City Center in 2004, and by then she was impressed. "The company just keeps getting fantastic dancers. To have Jorma as a resident choreographer is a big deal. He's not a middle-of-the-road choreographer. He's extreme. He's given the company an identity it has never had. Both he and Mikko are taking risks. I think that Mikko is stretching Jorma and that Jorma is stretching the dancers."

Mark Morris was also high on the company in the 2006–07 season. The nadir of his long association with Boston came when he withdrew a work from the company in the 1990s because its performances weren't up to his standards, wrote Louise Kennedy in an interview with Morris in the *Boston Globe.* He was lured back to Boston to create *Up and Down* in March 2006. "They had a very bad patch," Morris told Kennedy. "But Mikko's really moving it forward beautifully. I went to see *La Sylphide,* and it was so great I couldn't believe it."

With all Boston Ballet's troubles, Nissinen is ever the optimist. "My mission is to serve Terpsichore," the muse of the dance in ancient Greece. However, serving Terpsichore up to Nissinen's standards requires work at the highest level from many contributors: dancers who must perform classics with technical and artistic virtuosity while absorbing new material and presenting it with clarity and integrity; choreographers who, while working in the shadow of Balanchine, must find new means of using the exquisitely trained bodies and minds they work with to do what only ballet can; the directors, teachers, and répétiteurs who choose the dancers and the repertoire and ensure that it will be presented authentically and effectively; the musical staff, whose critical artistic contribution is seldom singled out for appreciation; the medical staff, who must minimize the effect of ballet's extraordinary demands on the superbly conditioned and trained bodies in their charge; the designers and other staff responsible for the trappings that turn those bodies into the

Pointe shoes. Photo by Wally Gilbert.

dramatic and magical creatures that appear onstage; the administrators who must make the whole operation run as smoothly as possible (hence Nissinen's remark on the trickle-down effect if he panics during a crisis); and trustees who must provide or find the wherewithal for all of this to happen.

Boston Ballet showed during the 2006–2007 season that it could meet both Terpsichore's and Nissinen's demands. Just before the gala that opened the company's season in the fall of 2008, the Ballet's board extended Nissinen's chances to realize his vision by renewing his contract through 2014. Whether the company will be able to continue to perform at the high standard he set, given the cuts he was forced to make earlier in 2008, will depend not only on the efforts of those described in this book but also on the audience, government, and corporate community, on whom the future of the arts in America also rests.

As a child, CHRISTINE TEMIN studied dance with Boston Ballet. She went on to study art history at Bryn Mawr College and both dance and art history at the University of North Carolina, where she earned an MFA in choreography. She taught ballet at Harvard University, Middlebury College, and Wellesley College before becoming dance and art critic for the *Boston Globe,* a position she held from 1978 to 2005. She is now a freelance writer on the subjects of dance and the visual arts.

WALLY GILBERT has had a long career in science and in business. He is the Carl M. Loeb University Professor Emeritus at Harvard University, where he was at various times a physicist, a biophysicist, a biochemist, and a molecular biologist. He was awarded a Nobel Prize in Chemistry in 1980 for his discovery of a rapid method to determine the sequence of the chemical groups in DNA. He has started a number of biotechnology companies and is now a partner in a venture capital firm, Bio-Technology Investors. He is currently pursuing a career in digital art and has had numerous one-man shows. He and Christine Temin were granted unprecedented access to Boston Ballet company rehearsals and performances.